PRAISE FOR
PERMANENCE

"Change isn't the hard part—it's *making it last* that is. *Permanence* gives you the tools and daily practices you need to finally stop slipping back into old patterns. This is a practical road map to lasting growth and the life you actually want."

—Mel Robbins, *New York Times* bestselling author of *The Let Them Theory* and host of *The Mel Robbins Podcast*

"Don't just read this book. Use it. Start tomorrow morning, before your enthusiasm fades and your excuses multiply. Pick your questions. Find your quiet moment. Begin the practice that will become a consistent, trusted engine of change."

—Michael Bungay Stanier, bestselling author of *The Coaching Habit* and *The Advice Trap*

"Six minutes.Two questions. Everything changes. Transformation isn't about elaborate systems or expensive solutions, but the radical simplicity of showing up for yourself daily. In *Permanence*, you'll discover a battle-tested practice that will disrupt your autopilot existence and allow you to scale the curve of your potential. Permanently."

—Whitney Johnson, CEO, Disruption Advisors; global top-ten management thinker, Thinkers50; *Wall Street Journal* bestselling author of *Smart Growth* and *Disrupt Yourself*

"*Permanence* is both profound and practical. It's also a joy to read. The authors show how small steps are the key to big change—and measuring is an essential part of nurturing growth. Ostensibly a guide to becoming a better person, this is really a book about leadership. To earn the right to lead others, start with this book."

—Amy C. Edmondson, Novartis Professor of Leadership, Harvard Business School; author of *Right Kind of Wrong: The Science of Failing Well*

"*Permanence* is a powerful reminder that real change doesn't come from big declarations—it comes from small, daily choices and consistent effort. Marshall Goldsmith's Daily Questions have helped countless leaders, including me, stay focused on becoming who they want to be. Lisa Broderick brings this process to life with clarity and heart. If you want to lead with intention and live with purpose, read this book."

—Garry Ridge, chairman emeritus, WD-40 Company; *USA Today* bestselling author, *Any Dumb-Ass Can Do It*

"I LOVE this book. In these pages are practical tools for you to become the person you want to be . . . and stay that way! Lisa and Marshall's teachings have changed my life, and I am a six-question addict! They are game changers. *Permanence* gets to the point and is easy to read and reread. It will make your life better, I promise. Treat yourself!"

—Chester Elton, bestselling author of *The Carrot Principle*, *Anxiety at Work*, and *Leading with Gratitude*

"Sustained success doesn't come from quick wins—you get there through intentional daily actions. This smart, practical guide shows you how to stay focused on what matters most, nurture meaningful growth, and create the future you want through consistent, purposeful effort."

—Dorie Clark, author of *The Long Game* and *Reinventing You*

"Changing behaviors that undermine us is easy, but maintaining change over time is hard. As resistance sets in, we revert to familiar patterns that feel hard-wired. That's why Lisa and Marshall's manual for sustaining positive behavioral change is such a breakthrough. It offers a practical, energizing, and time-tested way to become your best self—and to stay that way for the rest of your life."

—Sally Helgesen, author of *How Women Rise, Rising Together,* and *The Female Advantage*

"*Permanence* unlocks the secrets to sustainable change with the precision of a surgeon and the heart of an empath."

—Marcus Collins, award-winning cultural strategist and author of *For the Culture*

"*Permanence* is a clear, compelling guide to the hard—but essential—work of self-awareness, accountability, and lasting success. With practical tools like the Daily Question Process and feedforward, readers can focus on what fuels real growth: insightful reflection and purposeful action. A must-read for anyone serious about becoming—and staying—their best self."

—Dr. Tasha Eurich, organizational psychologist and *New York Times* bestselling author of *Shatterproof, Insight,* and *Bankable Leadership*

amplifypublishinggroup.com
publishing.100coaches.com

Permanence: Become the Person You Want to Be—and Stay That Way

For more information, please contact:
100 Coaches Publishing, an imprint of Amplify Publishing Group
620 Herndon Parkway, Suite 220
Herndon, VA 20170
info@amplifypublishing.com

Library of Congress Control Number: 2025909896

CPSIA Code: PRV0925A

ISBN-13: 979-8-89138-609-9

Printed in the United States

PERMANENCE

BECOME THE PERSON YOU WANT TO BE *AND STAY THAT WAY*

LISA BRODERICK
MARSHALL GOLDSMITH

Contents

Foreword ix

Chapter 1: How We Got Here 1

PART I
Foundations of Sustainable Change

Chapter 2: Self-Engagement Through Measurement 9
Chapter 3: Let's Talk About Us 27

PART II
The Power of Daily Reinforcement and Accountability

Chapter 4: Six Questions That Will Change Your Life 45
Chapter 5: The Obstacles to Daily Practice 61
Chapter 6: Measuring What Matters to You 73

PART III
Tools for Sustained Success

Chapter 7: Sustaining Mastery and Growth 89
Chapter 8: More Strategies for the Future You 101

Epilogue 119
Appendix: Supporting Studies and Research 121
Daily Questions Journal 123
About the Authors 153

Foreword

Here's the danger.

You're about to read a book and it will make perfect sense. You'll nod along, maybe take some notes. You'll think, "Yes, this is *exactly* what I need to do." And, sorry, then there's a decent chance you'll do nothing with it.

You're not alone, of course. We're both consumers of wisdom, collectors of insights, and hoarders of good intentions. We know what we *should* do. But so often, we don't.

The doing that this book is asking of you seems simple enough: Ask yourself better questions. Every day. Without fail.

I can attest that this works because this is one thing I do. Every morning, before the day gets its hooks into me, I sit with my journal and respond to three questions of my own. It takes maybe five minutes, often less.

Some days the answers flow; other days I'm just going through the motions. But I show up. Every day. And over time, those few minutes have become the foundation for everything else I do.

The simplicity is an essential part of its power.

We love the sound of complicated solutions. Sometimes we

believe that if the solution isn't elaborate, expensive, or exhausting, it can't possibly work.

But that's backward. The most profound changes have their source in the smallest, most mundane practices.

Marshall Goldsmith has spent decades coaching some of the world's most successful leaders, and on this he and I agree: The difference between people who change and people who stay stuck isn't intelligence, resources, or even motivation. It's the willingness to show up for themselves, day after day, with curiosity.

The questions you ask matter. "Did I do my best to set clear goals?" "Did I do my best to be happy?" "Did I do my best to build positive relationships?"

Notice the wording. Not "Did I achieve my goals?" or "Was I happy?" Rather, it's "Did I do my best?" This isn't about perfection; it's about effort. It's not about outcomes; it's about ownership.

Morning questions don't guarantee a perfect day, but they do initiate an intentional one.

The Daily Questions are a mirror. They reflect back the gap between who you are and who you want to be. They make the invisible visible. They turn vague intentions into concrete awareness.

So, as the heading says, you can do this.

Don't just read this book. Use it. Start tomorrow morning, before your enthusiasm fades and your excuses multiply. Pick your questions. Find your quiet moment.

Begin the practice that will become a consistent, trusted engine of change.

—Michael Bungay Stanier, bestselling author of *The Coaching Habit* and *The Advice Trap*

CHAPTER 1

How We Got Here

This book grew out of an inspiration that Marshall Goldsmith, one of the most influential executive coaches in the world, had in 2023 when he called me and said, "Lisa, I want you to do some research." He asked me to call a cohort of his clients every weekday for a year and ask them Daily Questions. You may be aware that Marshall's clients are among the greatest leaders in the world. Although these clients had been through a foundational coaching program with Marshall, they were not familiar with Daily Questions, which are Marshall's practice of daily accountability for achieving his most important goals. I'm an economist by education and now a coach. What's a better project than to collect a bunch of data from wildly successful people who were working on improving their lives? So I took down their names and contact information and headed off for a grand adventure. What I discovered was remarkable.

Over the course of the following year—through holidays and vacations, board meetings and last-minute appointments with heads of state—I called each of them on the phone every weekday. I listened to them, read the questions they'd written for themselves, and recorded their answers. With the exception of longer discussions around issues that called for coaching, this took all of about two minutes per phone call.

Their Daily Questions included Marshall's six recommended questions:

1. Did I do my best to set clear goals?
2. Did I do my best to make progress toward goal achievement?
3. Did I do my best to find meaning?
4. Did I do my best to be happy?
5. Did I do my best to build positive relationships?
6. Did I do my best to be fully engaged?

In addition, each of these leaders added their own questions that represented what was most important in their lives. This included things like, "How many minutes did I walk?" "How many push-ups?" "Did I say or do something nice for my wife, my husband, my son, my daughter?" One of the leaders' questions was, "Did I do my best to avoid angry or destructive comments about other people today?" The vast majority of leaders didn't respond yes to their Daily Questions until the last month of the research year—proving that, as simple as the questions are, they're hard for people to actually *do*.

During the research, the participants were fully in the driver's seat. They wrote the questions; they gave the answers. There was no judgment or asking why. They were simply being accountable to themselves. All I did was call them each day.

Why did the leaders participate in the research? In their own words: "Because I knew I needed something that went deeper than the normal 360"; "Because I was willing to try anything to get to a breakthrough"; "I figured it couldn't hurt"; and "I trusted Marshall."

What were some of the breakthroughs? "My breakthrough was that it allowed me to fully accept and lean into *my* purpose and vision for my job." "Being able to let go of resentment or a need for control over others." "My breakthrough was a sense of separation from the minutiae of day-to-day." "A reminder of the bigger purpose." "The ability to see the whole picture without judgment."

As for the responses to the questions recorded over the course of the year, they showed a noticeable trend over time, beginning the year with low and inconsistent scores for the first six months and progressing to consistent and nearly perfect scores for the last six months of the research year.

And when asked to share whatever they felt would benefit others to know, this was the response: The value of social connection cannot be overstated, with one leader commenting, "Just getting on the phone with you became a highlight of my day."

From Marshall's perspective, what was he trying to find out? First, he wanted to know if people would quit. In Marshall's prior research, half the people who start this Daily Questions practice quit within two weeks. And they do not quit because it doesn't work; they quit because it's hard to look in the mirror and evaluate yourself on a daily basis. And as hard as it is for us to admit, it's much easier to point out other people's faults than it is to face our own problems.

In the research I conducted, no one quit.

Second, Marshall wanted to know if people would get better and *stay* better. As you might expect, people did get better over time. In fact, about half the cohort are still doing the Daily Questions process to this day.

Everyone got better and stayed that way . . . as long as they kept doing it. I checked in with a few who stopped asking and answering Daily Questions after the year, and—not surprisingly—they reported setbacks on their prior progress.

The third result was a surprise. About halfway through the year, all of the people in the cohort reported the same phenomenon. They found themselves changing their behavior throughout the day, and they were doing this for two reasons. One, so they could spare themselves the shame and embarrassment of having to tell me they hadn't tried their best. And two, they remembered who they wanted to become in real time and adjusted accordingly.

Wow. Think about who these people are. Just because of this simple practice, some of the world's top leaders changed their behavior in real time throughout their workdays to become the people they wanted to be. Imagine a world where everyone did that. Marshall had come up with a simple way to actually get people to change, and it didn't take a ton of time.

This makes sense when you consider the entire body of Marshall's research over the years and what he's discovered—that meaningful change doesn't come from massive overhauls. Instead, it's built through small, consistent actions reinforced by accountability and collaboration. Time and again, research shows this, and that's why he shares it with so many people.

Through decades of coaching and working with top leaders, Marshall has analyzed what truly fuels long-term growth. He's pinpointed workplace habits that even the most successful leaders struggle with and developed practical methods to help them stay focused on what really matters. And at the core of all this research is a simple reality: Success isn't a fixed destination—it's an ongoing process that requires self-awareness, adaptability, and strong connections with others.

This book is the sum total of what Marshall taught me about how—and why—you should do this for yourself. It also contains a handy Daily Questions Journal at the back of the book so you can begin right away.

As Marshall would say, what are we waiting for? Let's get started.

—Lisa Broderick

PART I

Foundations of Sustainable Change

"I never arrived at the perfection I had been so ambitious of obtaining, but fell far short of it; yet I was, by the endeavor, a better and a happier man than I otherwise should have been if I had not attempted it."

— Benjamin Franklin

CHAPTER 2

Self-Engagement Through Measurement

Let's start with a simple idea: *Self-measurement changes everything.* It's such a straightforward concept—and it can unlock meaningful, lasting growth in ways that might seem unbelievable. Want to be better at something? Start measuring it. Consistently. Daily, if you can. By tracking even the smallest things you want to change, you'll create a road map for progress one step at a time. It'll take two minutes a day, cost you absolutely nothing, and help you get better at almost anything.

Now, some of you are skeptical of that. You think, *Two minutes a day, costs nothing, and helps me get better at almost anything? That sounds too good to be true.* Everything we're going to tell you is going to be incredibly easy to understand. What's difficult is to *keep doing it.*

What we've learned over the last many decades is that attention to the small stuff adds up to sustained success—if you take the two minutes a day to just keep track. If you do what's included here, you'll have tangible proof of your growth. And when you have that, a compelling feedback loop will kick in that will keep you going. It's like your own personal motivator for life.

Now, before you dismiss this as a self-help gimmick, let us share some stories of people who figured this out before now. These are not just anecdotes—they're life lessons.

Ancient Wisdom: Stoicism and Daily Reflection— The Original Self-Improvement System

The idea of tracking your progress and holding yourself accountable isn't new. People have been doing it for thousands of years. Long before structured self-improvement systems existed, the Stoics—Marcus Aurelius, Seneca, and Epictetus*—were refining daily practices to stay focused, disciplined, and aligned with their values.

Marcus Aurelius, one of Rome's greatest emperors, wrote down his thoughts every single day. He wasn't writing for an audience or trying to impress anyone. He was keeping himself on track, making sure his actions matched his values. That journal, now known as *Meditations*,† was his personal system for self-measurement. Today, it looks a lot like the modern practice of Daily Questions—checking in with yourself, reflecting on your behavior, and using that awareness to keep improving.

Seneca, a philosopher and statesman, made nightly reflection a core habit. Every evening, he asked himself simple but powerful questions: "What bad habit did I break today?" and "How am I better now?" He understood something important—small,

---

* Holiday, Ryan. 2016. *The Daily Stoic: 366 Meditations on Wisdom, Perseverance, and the Art of Living*. New York: Penguin.

† Aurelius, Marcus. (180 AD) 2019. *Meditations*. New York: Penguin.

measurable progress adds up. His method reinforced consistency and personal integrity, much like modern accountability frameworks do today.

Epictetus, another Stoic thinker, emphasized focusing only on what's within your control—your actions, your choices, and your responses. His philosophy cut through distractions and kept his energy directed at what actually mattered. That's the foundation of any good self-improvement practice: measuring what you can control and not wasting effort on things you can't.

Why This Still Works Today

The Stoics figured out three core principles that still hold up:

1. **Living with Purpose**: Marcus Aurelius believed that every action should be aligned with one's core values and greater purpose. His meditations were a daily reminder to act with integrity, discipline, and intention. By taking time to reflect on *why* we do what we do—not just *how*—we ensure that our growth isn't just about habits but about building a meaningful life.
2. **Consistent Reflection**: Seneca's nightly review process was about reinforcing self-awareness and ensuring steady progress. Taking a few minutes each day to assess your actions creates a continuous loop of self-improvement.
3. **Effort over Outcomes**: Epictetus taught that real empowerment comes from focusing on what you can control: your own actions. This is the same idea behind measuring effort instead of fixating on results.

Benjamin Franklin: Perfectly Imperfect Progress

Fast-forward a few centuries to one of our favorite historical figures—Benjamin Franklin. Founding Father, inventor, diplomat, and self-improvement enthusiast. That's right. Franklin wasn't just busy with lightning rods and revolutions; he was also one of the earliest champions of what we'd now call habit-tracking. And, like with so much of what he did, he did it with diligence and a healthy dose of practicality.

At just twenty years old, Franklin came up with a plan to live his best life by focusing on what he called the "thirteen virtues." These weren't vague ideas like, "Try to be a good person." No, Franklin liked specifics—things like *temperance*, *order*, and *humility*. Each virtue was tied to a behavior, and he created a system to keep track of how well he practiced them all.

And he wasn't alone. According to several of the Founding Fathers, the "path to happiness" didn't include chasing after fleeting pleasures.* They believed true happiness came from pursuing virtue. In their view, that meant dedicating yourself to self-improvement, building character, and living with a sense of moral purpose. They weren't talking about quick fixes or surface-level stuff. They were talking about actively cultivating good habits, practicing self-discipline, and striving to be better every day. To them, happiness was deeply tied to liberty—being able to govern yourself and live with integrity. That's the kind of lasting fulfillment they were aiming for, and honestly, we think there's a lot we can learn from that mindset today.

---

* Rosen, Jeffrey. 2024. *The Pursuit of Happiness: How Classical Writers on Virtue Inspired the Lives of the Founders and Defined America.* New York: Simon & Schuster.

Now, here's where Franklin's insight really matters for our purposes: He didn't aim for perfection. He knew he'd slip up. So he focused on progress, one day and one virtue at a time. And he measured that progress—every single day.

The Original Habit-Tracker

Franklin's method wasn't complicated; it was, however, ingenious. He carried a little notebook with a grid—virtues listed down one side and days of the week across the top. Every evening, he'd sit down and reflect on how he'd done that day, marking any lapses with a small dot. If he gossiped, he'd note it under "silence." If he let his workspace get messy, a dot went under "cleanliness."

He would focus his energy on one virtue per week and tracked all thirteen over time. And when the week ended? He'd review his progress, think about what went well, and move on to the next virtue. He was like a one-man performance review, only gentler and without the threat of an HR intervention.

What's remarkable here isn't just the system—it's the mindset. Franklin wasn't trying to beat himself up. He wasn't aiming to become the perfect human. He was simply trying to get a little better each day.

A Virtuous Diplomat

Let's think about how this played out in his life. Imagine Franklin in eighteenth-century Paris as a diplomat, surrounded by indulgent French society—feasts, fine wine, and no shortage of women. Most people might have gotten caught up in the glamour, but Franklin? He had his virtues. He didn't need to pull out his notebook in the middle of a state dinner. The principles he'd worked on were already embedded in his character.

His commitment to things like humility and sincerity made him someone people felt they could trust. And in diplomacy, trust is paramount. The alliances he helped secure with France during the American Revolution didn't just happen by chance; they happened because Franklin showed up as a person who practiced trustworthiness. He was reliable and focused on the bigger picture.

Imperfection by Design

Here's our favorite part of Franklin's story: He openly admitted he never mastered all thirteen virtues. And that's not a failure—it's the point. As Franklin himself wrote, "I was, by the endeavor, a better and a happier man than I otherwise should have been if I had not attempted it."*

Self-engagement through measurement isn't about arriving at perfection. Instead, it teaches you how to become a little kinder, more disciplined, or more present than you were the day before. Franklin's grid wasn't a scoreboard; it was a tool for reflection and growth.

---

* Franklin, Benjamin and Louis P. Masur. 2016. *The Autobiography of Benjamin Franklin: With Related Documents*. Boston: Bedford/St. Martin's, Macmillan Learning.

Franklin's Lessons for Us

So, what can we learn from Franklin? First, change doesn't have to be overwhelming. His virtues system shows us that small, deliberate actions—when practiced consistently—can add up to something meaningful. Here's how you can channel your inner Franklin:

1. **Choose What Matters**: Like Franklin's virtues, decide on a few habits or values that resonate with you. Write them down. Keep them simple.
2. **Measure It**: Whether you use a journal, a spreadsheet, or a pack of sticky notes, track how you're doing. The act of measuring keeps you going.
3. **Expect Imperfection**: You're going to have some misses you'll record in your data, and that's okay. The goal is progress, not perfection.

A Timeless Legacy

Franklin's virtues system is as relevant today as it was in the 1700s. If you've ever felt overwhelmed by the idea of change, Franklin's approach reminds us that improvement doesn't happen in sudden, huge changes—it happens in small, measured steps.

So, the next time you think you need to overhaul your life in an afternoon, take a page out of Franklin's gridded notebook: Start small. Track your progress. Celebrate your wins, no matter how tiny they seem. Your version of Franklin's notebook might not make you a Founding Father, but it just might make you a better and happier person.

Bridging Ancient Wisdom and Modern Practice

The Stoics and Ben Franklin weren't the only ones who understood the power of daily reflection. Fast-forward a few more centuries, and their ideas are still influencing how people think about self-improvement. One modern author who helped bring daily self-reflection into the mainstream is Ryan Holiday. In *The Daily Stoic*,* Holiday takes the core ideas of Marcus Aurelius, Seneca, and Epictetus and makes them practical and accessible. His emphasis on daily journaling and self-reflection mirrors the Daily Questions process, reinforcing the idea that small, consistent check-ins drive real, lasting change.

One of Holiday's key messages is focusing only on what we can control—our actions, choices, and responses. This aligns with Daily Questions, which shift attention to effort rather than outcomes. Another major theme in his work is *memento mori*, or remembering that life is finite. Holiday argues that when we keep this perspective in mind, we gain clarity on what truly matters and ensure that our daily actions reflect our priorities. His approach emphasizes that real success isn't about external achievements; it's about character, integrity, and living in alignment with personal values. He also highlights the Stoic practice of responding deliberately rather than reacting impulsively, which builds emotional resilience over time.

The key takeaway is that meaningful personal growth doesn't come from occasional big efforts. It comes from consistent, structured reflection; small, measurable improvements; and daily reinforcement of what truly matters. Progress isn't about perfection—it's about steady steps forward.

---

* Holiday, Ryan. 2016. *The Daily Stoic: 366 Meditations on Wisdom, Perseverance, and the Art of Living*. New York: Penguin.

More Modern Amplifications

Other modern thinkers take these ideas in different directions. James Clear, in *Atomic Habits*, explores how identity is shaped by small, consistent actions. He describes each choice as "a vote for the person you wish to become." We love this concept, which echoes Daily Questions, where the focus is on effort rather than just chasing outcomes. Tracking actions, being intentional, and maintaining consistency are essential for long-term growth.

Tim Ferriss, author of *The 4-Hour Workweek*,* looks at self-improvement from a different angle, emphasizing structured reflection across multiple time frames—daily, weekly, monthly, and annually. He asks questions like, "What's one thing I'm avoiding that, if tackled, would simplify everything else?" and "Am I investing time in activities that produce disproportionate results?" While Daily Questions keep the focus on day-to-day alignment, Ferriss's approach encourages zooming out to see the bigger picture. Both methods reinforce the same idea: Real growth happens through structured reflection and consistent self-awareness.

Whether it's tracking daily habits, reflecting on long-term priorities, or simply striving for incremental improvement, these modern thinkers offer practical ways to get where you want to go.

Pre-Suasion and Daily Questions

Another really interesting concept that connects with Daily Questions comes from Robert Cialdini's book *Pre-Suasion*.†

---

* Ferriss, Timothy. 2007. *The 4-Hour Workweek: Escape 9-5, Live Anywhere, and Join the New Rich*. New York: Crown.

† Cialdini, Robert B. 2016. *Pre-Suasion: A Revolutionary Way to Influence and Persuade*. New York: Simon & Schuster.

Cialdini explores how the moments leading up to a choice influence the outcome, and this is exactly what Daily Questions do. By setting the intention to measure effort each day, they help direct focus toward what truly matters.

Cialdini emphasizes *channeled attention*—the idea that what we focus on before making a decision significantly impacts what we ultimately choose. When we repeatedly bring attention to the behaviors we want to cultivate, they become a natural part of our lives. He also highlights the power of *framing questions*. The way a question is asked shapes the response. This small shift—focusing on effort instead of results—reinforces personal responsibility and long-term growth.

Commitment consistency is another key principle in Cialdini's work. Once we commit to something, we are more likely to follow through. This helps explain why a structured process like Daily Questions works so well—it reinforces commitment and makes it easier to sustain positive behaviors over time.

Cialdini also discusses *self-relevant cues*—small reminders that reinforce identity. Daily Questions serve this purpose by keeping our goals and values front and center. Over time, they strengthen self-image, helping individuals see themselves as intentional, self-aware, and committed to personal growth.

Finally, Cialdini introduces the idea of *privileged moments*—times when we are particularly open to influence. By encouraging reflection at the same time each day, Daily Questions create conditions for lasting change. Habitual self-reflection turns into an ongoing system for better decision-making, continuous progress, and alignment with core values.

The through line of all these approaches—ancient to modern—is that real change doesn't come from external rewards or occasional big efforts. It comes from paying attention to the small things, measuring what matters, and making consistent, intentional choices. That's the formula for lasting success.

Peter Drucker: What Gets Measured Gets Managed

To understand how this all ties back to our work, we need to share the story of how Marshall first met Peter Drucker. If you don't know Peter Drucker, he's considered the father of modern management, and many of his ideas have enormously shaped the worlds of business, management, and leadership as we know them today. Picture Marshall as a young professor attending a management conference where Drucker was the keynote speaker. Drucker's talk was, of course, brilliant. And afterward, Marshall was determined to meet him.

Now, of course, Marshall was too young to be important to Drucker. But he went up anyway, introduced himself, and told Drucker how much he admired his work. You know what Drucker did? He didn't talk about himself. He didn't bask in praise. Instead, Drucker turned the conversation around and asked Marshall about his work, his goals, and what he wanted to do. Think about that: Here's this legendary figure, and he's showing genuine interest in some young guy who just walked up to him.

And then, Drucker said this: "We spend a lot of time teaching leaders what to do. We don't spend enough time teaching leaders what to stop." That idea was so profound, yet so obvious. How many of us get stuck trying to do more and more instead of stepping back and asking, "What should I *stop* doing?" That's one of the most powerful things we can do as leaders: let go of the habits and behaviors that hold us back.

From Vague Goals to Tangible Progress

Drucker also had a simple saying: "What gets measured gets managed." And he was right. Whether you're managing a business or your own habits, the act of measuring turns vague aspirations into concrete actions.

On the surface, Drucker's theory might sound like business-speak. When you dig into it, you'll see it's a universal truth that applies to just about every aspect of life. Whether you're running a global company or just trying to become a better version of yourself, measurement is the bridge between intention and action. It's the antidote to the vagueness that so often derails our best-laid plans.

Let's break it down. Imagine your goal is to become a better listener. What does that even mean? You could nod your head while someone else is talking. That doesn't mean you're improving. Now consider Drucker's golden rule. To measure your progress, you could track specific behaviors: How often did you make eye contact during conversations today? How many times today did you ask a genuine follow-up question? On the flip side, how often did you tune out the other person and talk over them? These are measurable actions that bring clarity to an otherwise nebulous goal.

Turning Data into Progress

Drucker believed that measurement is more than just a management tool—it's a mechanism for focus and accountability. When we measure something, we pay attention to it. And when we pay attention, we naturally start to manage it more effectively. It's like having a compass that keeps you moving toward your destination even when the going gets rough.

Here's the point of measuring personal growth: It creates the feedback loop we described earlier. When you see that you've maintained eye contact in 80 percent of your conversations this week, it's a win that motivates you to keep going. And if you only get to 50 percent, that's valuable information too. It's not failure; it's data. Measurement doesn't just tell you how you're doing; it tells you what to work on, where to focus, and how to improve.

Drucker's insight reminds us that clarity is power. Goals without measurement are like New Year's resolutions: easy to make, hard to keep. When you measure, you manage. Every day can be a fresh start. You don't give up; you try again. You move from dreaming to doing, from wishing to achieving. Whether you're leading a team or leading yourself, it's a principle that stands the test of time. If it worked for Drucker's Fortune 500 clients (and it did), it can work for you too.

Banking Your Wins

If there's one lesson to take from these great thinkers, it's this: Personal growth isn't about grand transformations—it's about small, consistent actions that add up over time. From the Stoics to Franklin, and from Drucker to modern behavioral experts, they all point to a simple truth: What gets measured gets improved. Self-measurement isn't just about tracking yourself; it's about sustaining momentum, building resilience, and making sure your daily actions align with what matters.

Think of self-measurement as a bank account. Every time you make a choice that aligns with your values—whether it's reflecting on your day like Marcus Aurelius, marking a progress check like Franklin, or measuring the impact of your habits like James Clear—you're making a deposit. These aren't grand gestures; they're tiny deposits. Over time, those moments add up. They create a reserve of confidence and resilience you can draw upon when things don't go as planned. And things definitely won't always go as planned.

We've seen this play out time and time again, both in our lives and in the lives of the leaders we coach. The ones who consistently succeed aren't the ones waiting for monumental wins to validate them. They're the ones who know how to celebrate their everyday wins. Did they get through a tough meeting with grace? That's a win. Did they take five minutes to show appreciation to a colleague? Another win. These small actions are the building blocks of a happy and fulfilling life.

This is a simple yet powerful idea—to align your daily actions with your bigger values. It's not a question of being perfect. No one's perfect. The point of this alignment is showing up each day and focusing on what matters most. We measure these things because *they matter to us*. When we see those small wins adding up, we know we're making progress. And when we fall short, we use that feedback to adjust and improve. Tracking those moments, no matter how small, creates a powerful feedback loop that reminds us who we are and what we're aiming for.

Let's be honest: There's no point in waiting for life's big wins to feel validated. That's a recipe for disappointment. Instead, bank the small stuff. These moments are meaningful, and they create a foundation of strength we can rely on when the going gets tough.

So don't overlook the small wins. Recognize them. Celebrate them. Bank them. Because when you do, you're not just creating a record of progress—you're building a more purposeful, resilient version of yourself. And trust us: That's worth every deposit.

Begin Building Your Self-Measurement Framework

Thinking about doing it? Here's how you can start building your own self-measurement system:*

1. **Define What You Want to Improve**
   Choose specific areas of your life to focus on—whether it's productivity, relationships, health, or emotional resilience. Be clear about what matters most so you can track meaningful progress.

2. **Create a Simple Tracking System**
   Use a notebook, spreadsheet, or habit-tracking app to log your progress. Keep it structured but easy to maintain, like Benjamin Franklin's grid system or a checklist with key behaviors you want to reinforce daily.

---

* Note that at the back of this book, you'll find your very own Daily Questions Journal with room for two weeks' worth of answers.

3. **Ask Yourself Questions Each Day**
   Develop a set of reflective questions that keep you accountable, such as:

   - *Did I do my best to stay focused today?*
   - *Did I make progress on my most important goal?*
   - *Did I show up for the people who matter to me?*

   Frame questions around effort rather than outcomes to keep momentum strong.

4. **Set a Time for Reflection**
   Dedicate a few minutes each day—morning or evening—to review your responses. Marcus Aurelius and Seneca practiced this to reinforce self-awareness. The key is consistency, even if it's just two minutes a day.

5. **Adjust Based on Patterns**
   After tracking for a week or two, look for trends. If certain areas consistently fall short, adjust your approach. Maybe you need a new strategy or more realistic expectations. Use setbacks as data for improvement rather than as reasons to stop.

6. **Hold Yourself Accountable with a Partner**
   Share your self-measurement practice with a friend, coach, or mentor. Having someone check in with you—even informally—reinforces commitment. Mutual accountability increases the likelihood of sustaining the habit over time.

Forget Perfection; Focus on Progress

Here's the deal: We can all be better. Self-measurement doesn't require massive effort; it just requires consistency. So start small. Track one thing. Then another. Over time, you'll build a feedback loop that drives improvement while also reminding you what you're capable of.

And that's self-measurement: It shows you that progress is always within reach—one step, one measurement, one moment at a time.

WHERE to Begin

1. Define What You Want to Improve

Choose specific areas of your life to focus on—whether it's productivity, relationships, health, or emotional resilience. Be clear about what matters most.

2. Create a Simple Tracking System

Use a notebook, spreadsheet, or habit-tracking app to log your progress. Keep it structured but easy to maintain, like Benjamin Franklin's grid system or a checklist with key behaviors you want to reinforce daily.

3. Ask Yourself Questions Each Day

Develop a set of reflective questions that keep you accountable, such as:

1. Did I do my best to stay focused today?
2. Did I make progress on my most important goal?
3. Did I show up for the people who matter to me?

4. Set a Time for Reflection

Dedicate a few minutes each day—morning or evening—to review your responses. Marcus Aurelius and Seneca practiced this to reinforce self-awareness. The key is consistency, even if it's just two minutes a day.

5. Adjust Based on Patterns

After tracking for a week or two, look for trends. If certain areas consistently fall short, adjust your approach. Maybe you need a new strategy or more realistic expectations. Use setbacks as data for improvement.

6. Hold Yourself Accountable with a Partner

Share your self-measurement practice with a friend, coach, or mentor. Mutual accountability increases the likelihood of sustaining the habit over time.

CHAPTER 3

Let's Talk About Us

Many of you already know Marshall; he'll tell you he's from a small town in Kentucky called Valley Station. He studied at Indiana University, where he discovered his passion for both learning and teaching. That passion led Marshall to UCLA, where he earned his PhD, became a college professor, and then became a dean while he was still in his twenties.

What he's most known for, though, is executive coaching. When Marshall was teaching as a professor, he loved it. And then something happened that led him to coaching. An unexpected meeting with Dr. Paul Hersey, one of the brilliant minds behind Situational Leadership, changed the course of his life forever. Dr. Hersey invited Marshall to work with him after Hersey became double-booked. His offer? "Can you do what I do?" Marshall wasn't sure and said, "I'll give it a try." When Hersey offered to pay Marshall $1,000 a day—a huge amount of money compared to his $15,000-a-year professor's salary—he jumped at the chance. Marshall's first gig was a training session for Metropolitan Life Insurance in New York, and it went so well they said, "Send Marshall again!" That's how Marshall accidentally became a coach.

You may not know that in the 1970s business leaders were ashamed to say they worked with a coach. They thought it made them look weak or like they couldn't handle the pressures of success. Today, they are not seen as weak. And we like to think we may have helped that shift a bit. One thing we've tried to do is change the perception of coaching from "fix the loser" to "help the winner." We've worked really hard at that, and we're proud that coaching now has a very different image.

Some of the world's most accomplished leaders have been Marshall's clients. Here's what's important: We've learned far more from coaching them than they have from us. Coaching teaches humility. Having all the answers isn't the main issue; asking the right questions is what's important.

Finally, there's writing. Marshall's twenty-third book, *What Got You Here Won't Get You There*, became a bestseller after twenty-two others were read mostly by friends and relatives. Marshall will tell you it felt really good to write a book that someone finally bought! That book has been translated into thirty languages and has sold 1.2 million copies. Then Marshall's thirty-sixth book, *Triggers*, also became a *New York Times* and *Wall Street Journal* bestseller. So Marshall kept his hand at writing long enough to eventually succeed. Writing has also been his way of giving back to a broader audience by sharing the lessons learned with his clients.

As for me, I graduated with a degree in economics from Stanford University decades ago and then spent more than thirty years as a CEO, mostly for high-tech companies. These days, I'm a coach to other CEOs and business leaders, helping them become the best people they can be.

Which brings us to now. We want to share the power of simple self-reflection. If there's one important thing we can convey to you, it's this. For whatever level of success you've achieved in your life, know this: Real change begins and ends with self-reflection. And if you don't find ways to keep doing it, you won't stay successful. That's what we've built our careers on: helping people bridge the gap between who they are now and who they want to become so they can find meaning and happiness in their lives. We never arrive, and we always have room to improve.

Why Self-Reflection Matters

We've both worked with a lot of successful people, and here's what we've noticed: Most of them think they know themselves pretty well. What they don't always realize is how their behaviors impact the people around them. It's like this blind spot that keeps them stuck, and they don't even see it. Real growth starts when we really get honest about what drives us and how our actions line up with our values and goals.

That can be hard to accept, especially for high achievers. Many of us assume that if we're getting results now, everything else will fall into place in the future. The bottom line is, the skills that get us to today's success—drive, ambition, a laser focus on results—may not be the same ones that help us sustain it. In fact, if not balanced with humility, courage, and adaptability, these same traits can hold us back. This realization is at the heart of the matter: *Moving from where you are to where you want to be takes ongoing self-reflection.* And if you're not actively working on getting better, you're probably getting worse.

The Story of Matt

Here's a story about Matt. Matt runs one of the biggest restaurant empires in America—everything from fast food to mid-level fine dining. The guy's sharp, hardworking, and deeply invested in his team. He manages by walking around—watching everything from burger flipping to back-office operations. Matt would probably tell you he knows himself pretty well—and in many ways, he does. Recently, though, he came to a realization that shifted his approach to leadership: Success isn't just about hitting goals or having all the answers—it's about building strong relationships and being fully present with the people around you.

For years, Matt prided himself on being hands-on, walking the floors, and staying involved in the details of his business. He continued to do all of those things as the company grew, causing him to spend even more time behind the scenes. The business was growing, but he was spreading himself thin. He started to notice something: Despite all his effort, there was a growing disconnect between him and his team. Meetings didn't feel as productive as they could be, communication felt strained at times, and morale wasn't where he wanted it to be. And because he had always been so invested in his team, people noticed everything about him, including his newly reduced level of engagement. Some even thought he might be unhappy with their work because of the way he was acting.

Now, here's where it gets interesting. One day, one of his direct reports actually spoke up about it, asking if Matt was unhappy with their work. Can you imagine how that felt? Matt was taken aback. He'd been working his tail off to make the company better, and his team was taking it an entirely different way.

That's when it dawned on him. If he wanted to continue to build the company, the problem wasn't about strategy or operations—it was about relationships. He had been so focused on the business itself that he wasn't always making time to cultivate the relationships that held it all together. Sure, he was in the room, but he wasn't always *fully* present—listening, engaging, and connecting in a way that made people feel valued and understood and allowed them to contribute their best work.

That realization was a wake-up call. Matt decided to make a change. He committed to prioritizing the people around him by building stronger, more positive relationships and staying fully engaged in every interaction. To hold himself accountable, he started using Marshall's process of Daily Questions.

Every evening, Matt asked himself:

1. *Did I do my best to build meaningful connections with my team today?*
2. *Did I do my best to stay fully present in my conversations?*
3. *Did I do my best to support my team and show appreciation for their work?*

He even began having his assistant call him at the end of each day to ask these questions, have him rate himself on a scale of one to ten, and track his answers in a simple spreadsheet. The point wasn't to be perfect—it was to notice patterns and make consistent progress.

Over time, Matt saw a real difference. As he focused on being more present and engaged, his team felt heard, motivated, and appreciated. Meetings became more productive, trust deepened, and morale improved across the board. By nurturing those relationships and showing up fully for his people, Matt not only strengthened his leadership but also inspired his team to do their best work.

Here's what Matt learned: Success isn't always about hitting the numbers or implementing ideas. Equally important are the connections you build and the way you make others feel. By being fully present and engaged, you create an environment where everyone can thrive. And in the end, that's what real leadership is all about.

The Power of Intrinsic Motivation

Throughout our careers, we've seen the difference between people who chase external validation and those driven by intrinsic motivation. Those who pursue success for the sake of success often hit a ceiling. They end up feeling trapped and frustrated, unable to reach that next level of accomplishment. On the other hand, people who define success by their own values tend to sustain it and find more happiness along the way. Shifting from external validation to internal motivation is another key to long-term success.

One of Marshall's former clients, Frances Hesselbein, was the CEO of the Girl Scouts of the USA. Her leadership wasn't about personal achievement; it was about service and purpose. Her work reminds us that when we root our goals in intrinsic motivation, success becomes not just sustainable; it becomes deeply fulfilling. We'll talk more about Frances later on.

Intrinsic motivation—our inner drive to chase goals that are truly meaningful—keeps us engaged, adaptive, and resilient. It's why we've built our coaching approach around helping people focus on *what matters to them*, not just what they want to compare to others. When we're grounded in our own values, we're clearer about our goals, more resilient through setbacks, and able to keep moving forward.

Feedback Matters

One of the most important tools for self-awareness—and one of the hardest to master—is feedback. Feedback has always been with us. The first man who knelt by a pool to drink and saw his reflection experienced feedback in its rawest form. Formal feedback, like suggestion boxes or employee performance reviews, came much later. In every form and at every stage of history, feedback has been vital to self-reflection and understanding.

One type of feedback that we've often used is 360-degree feedback. This process collects input from people who work with, around, and for someone to give them a holistic view of how they're perceived. It remains one of the best methods we've found for helping successful people identify areas for growth.

Here's the issue: People often resist feedback. Why? They're delusional about their accomplishments. Studies show that upward of 90 percent of people consistently believe they are better than their peer group.* At the same time, it's psychologically real. Combine that with the natural reluctance of others to *give* negative feedback—especially to powerful leaders—and you see why feedback rarely breaks through.

Feedback works best when it's part of a reciprocal process where everyone, including the person providing feedback, commits to improving.

---

* Hoorens, Vera. "Self-enhancement and Superiority Biases in Social Comparison." *European Review of Social Psychology* 4, no. 1 (1993): 113–139. https://www.tandfonline.com/doi/abs/10.1080/14792779343000040.

A Story About Feedback

One of Marshall's most powerful personal lessons about feedback came when he was a twenty-eight-year-old PhD student at UCLA. He was in a small seminar led by Dr. Bob Tannenbaum, a revered psychologist and the man who invented the term "sensitivity training." The seminar could be described as an "encounter group" where they were encouraged to discuss anything they wanted.

For three weeks, Marshall spoke up in class discussions, offering comments about the people of Los Angeles. Sequined jeans, gold Rolls-Royces, manicured mansions—Marshall had plenty of criticisms. At the time, he thought he was making profound points about society.

Then, one day, Dr. Tannenbaum asked Marshall, "Who are you talking to?"

Marshall stammered, "The group."

He pressed, "But you're only looking at one person. Who is that?"

Marshall realized it was Dr. Tannenbaum he had been looking at.

"And why are you so concerned about impressing me?" asked Dr. Tannenbaum.

That question hit like a punch to the gut. For weeks, Marshall had been offering criticisms of other people he saw as obsessed with impressing others while doing exactly the same thing. It was a humbling moment, and it can be summed up in two profound insights:

1. It's easier to see flaws in others than in ourselves.
2. What we deny about ourselves is often glaringly obvious to others.

Daily Self-Measurement: Small Steps to Big Changes

So Marshall began using tools like 360-degree feedback to help executives understand how they were seen by others. And today we both use this tool to help with understanding and reflection because awareness is the first step toward progress. Over the years, we've found that it isn't enough to have occasional breakthroughs. Awareness is only the start of the process. Maintaining any change comes from something simpler: daily self-measurement. So now we encourage clients to use "micro-measurements"—small actions they can track every day—to build on their self-knowledge. It could be as simple as asking, "Did I really listen today?" or "Did I take a moment to express appreciation?" This practice may seem insignificant. Over time, however, it can bring about meaningful shifts. Marshall has worked with hundreds of the most successful CEOs and leaders in the world. That coaching may help them reach new heights, but only daily accountability keeps them there.

What matters isn't gathering data or achieving a perfect score. What matters is staying aware in a way that keeps us grounded in our values and goals. By asking ourselves simple questions regularly, we stay focused on the behaviors we want to embody, closing the gap between where we are and where we want to be. This process of self-reflection allows us to make course corrections without losing momentum.

The Story of Elena

Here's a story about Elena. Elena is the CEO of a major computer hardware company. This company's a big deal—cutting-edge processors, sleek designs, the works. Elena started in telecommunications and moved into high tech and the C-suite. She's brilliant, creative, and full of energy. If you met her, you'd instantly feel that spark. She's always brainstorming ways to keep the company ahead of the competition. Recently, she learned something important about herself—something a lot of successful people miss.

Elena came up with a performance-tracking system for her team. Simple, clear, effective—a traffic-light model. Green means everything's running smoothly, yellow flags minor issues, and red means critical challenges. At first, it worked beautifully. The production lines became more efficient, and deadlines were met. Elena was thrilled.

Then came a hiccup. In one of the monthly reviews, the team flagged a project as yellow because of supply chain delays. Elena, always the problem solver, casually said, "What if we try a new component from a different supplier? It might speed things up." She didn't think much of it—it was just an idea. To her team, though, it was an order. They shifted focus, redirected resources, and started integrating the new supplier's components.

Fast-forward to the next review, and the project status had gone red. Elena was shocked. "What happened?" she asked. The operations manager explained, "We prioritized the supplier change you suggested, and it set us back." Elena was floored. "Wait, that was just a suggestion. I didn't mean for you to change everything!"

This was a big moment for Elena. She saw something many of us don't: the gap between *what we think we're doing* and *how others experience it*. Elena thought she was inspiring creativity. Her team thought she was giving orders. That's when she started thinking, *How can I align my actions with my intentions and values?*

Elena decided to turn the traffic-light system inward. She began tracking her own leadership habits—things like how she communicated, framed suggestions, and clarified her intentions. She set up her own "lights": green for clear directives, yellow for ideas that could be misinterpreted, and red for behaviors that caused confusion.

Every day, Elena asked herself a few simple questions:

1. *Did I do my best to clarify my expectations today?*
2. *Did I do my best to communicate in a way that reflects my values?*
3. *Did I do my best to stay aligned with my goals?*

Here's what's important about this approach—it's not a question of being perfect. It's a question of staying aware. By asking herself these questions, Elena could spot patterns. She noticed when she was getting in her own way or confusing her team. She started pausing before tossing out ideas, saying things like, "What do you think we should do to fix this?" And when she didn't communicate clearly, she could course correct without losing momentum.

Over time, the results were incredible. Projects stayed on track. Her team felt more empowered and less confused. And here's the kicker: Elena didn't just measure herself to collect data or hit a perfect score. She did it to stay grounded in her values and goals. By reflecting on her behavior, she closed the gap between where she was and where she wanted to be—not just as a leader but as a person.

Daily self-measurement isn't the same as beating yourself up or chasing perfection. The difference is awareness. It's about staying focused on the behaviors that matter most to you and making small adjustments along the way. That's how Elena stayed aligned with her values while leading her company to even greater success. That's how all of us can keep moving forward: one question at a time.

Your Growth Mindset

Over the years, we've learned that one of the greatest strengths any of us can develop is a growth mindset. A fixed mindset believes that we're largely unchangeable—that we are who we are. A growth mindset says that we can change. This is the belief that, no matter our current achievements, there's always room to grow. It takes humility and a willingness to listen, especially when the feedback is tough. In our work, we teach people to see feedback as an opportunity, not as a critique.

We've noticed that, like athletes who constantly aim to improve, business professionals can gain a lot from a commitment to learning. This doesn't mean changing yourself with every bit of feedback or aiming for perfection. It's more about recognizing that growth is continual and that success is something we shape by refining our skills, attitudes, and goals over time.

Your Journey, Your Success

This isn't just for executives or those already at the top. It's for anyone who wants to make their daily life more meaningful. Whether you're a manager, an entrepreneur, or just starting out, the practices of self-reflection, humility, and constant growth can support all of us. By building a habit of daily reflection, tapping into intrinsic motivation, and staying aligned with your values, you'll never get stuck. You'll stay successful as you grow and enjoy the ride.

We tell these stories because they show that growth is an ongoing process—one that takes humility, curiosity, and a commitment to self-development. If there's one thing we've learned, it's that real, sustainable success is rooted in a desire to keep learning, adapting, and improving day by day. Our hope is that you'll discover that success has never been about reaching a destination—it's always been about meaning, happiness, *and* achievement.

Your life is your greatest project. Make it a good one.

SIMPLE

Self-Measurement

1. Embrace Honest Self-Reflection

- Understand your actions, their alignment with values, and their impact on others.
- Acknowledge that the skills for initial success might not sustain long-term growth.

2. Cultivate Intrinsic Motivation

- Shift from chasing external validation to pursuing goals rooted in personal values.
- Focus on autonomy, purpose, and mastery for lasting fulfillment.

3. Seek and Use Feedback

Embrace feedback as a tool for self-awareness and growth.

Participate in reciprocal feedback processes like 360-degree evaluations.

4. Practice Daily Self-Measurement

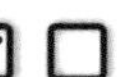

Track small, actionable behaviors daily (e.g., "Did I listen today?").

Use micro-measurements to stay focused and make consistent progress.

5. Adopt a Growth Mindset

See feedback as an opportunity for improvement, not criticism.

Commit to learning and refining skills over time without aiming for perfection.

6. Align Actions with Values

Regularly reflect on goals and behaviors to ensure they align with your core values.

Recognize that sustainable success is rooted in continuous growth and self-development.

PART II

The Power of Daily Reinforcement and Accountability

"Follow effective action with quiet reflection. From the quiet reflection will come even more effective action."

— Peter Drucker

CHAPTER 4

Six Questions That Will Change Your Life

Over the years, we've had the privilege of coaching some of the most successful leaders in the world—people who have achieved incredible milestones in their fields. All of them have been serious about setting meaningful goals for personal change. If there's one thing we've learned from them and taught to them, it's this: To get better at whatever you want to do or be, you have to take responsibility every single day. Personal growth doesn't happen when you wait for the stars to align or for someone else to hand you the magic formula. It happens when you take control of your own life one small step at a time. That's why we want to tell you about a simple process that takes just two minutes a day, costs absolutely nothing, and has the power to profoundly improve almost any aspect of your life. We call it the Daily Questions process. At first glance, it might seem too basic, too straightforward to have a real impact. But as anyone who's committed to it will tell you, this modest little practice can be life-changing.

Let's be up front, though—it's not easy to stick with, even though it's simple to understand. In fact, about half the people who try it quit within two weeks. Why? Not because it doesn't work, but precisely because it does. It works by holding up a mirror to your habits, your choices, and your actions every single day. And believe us when we say embracing that kind of accountability takes guts. It requires humility and a willingness to confront the truth about yourself—not just once but consistently. The process is both a discipline and a challenge, and it's also one of the most effective tools for self-improvement we've ever come across.

The inspiration for this process came to Marshall a few years ago when he was attending a presentation at the National Academy of Human Resources. He went with one of their fellows, and the other people attending were mostly heads of HR at big companies with a few outside consultants tossed in. The topic was employee engagement, and some of the brightest minds in HR were there, sharing strategies to boost engagement.

You know the term "employee engagement"? It's a big deal today, something most leaders have spent time learning and reading about. So, they presented this study and then talked about what companies should do. Things like increasing recognition, reward programs, good compensation, and training. It was all common sense stuff. Then they said, in spite of everything companies had been trying, total employee engagement was near an all-time low in the United States. The US was right at the bottom in terms of its own history of employee engagement!

Marshall listened to this and thought, *Wait a minute. If you all know so much and all this stuff works so well, why is employee engagement bottoming out? Why isn't it getting any better?* Then Marshall realized that 100 percent of the discussion around this topic was *what can the company do for its employees* and absolutely 0 percent was *what can employees do for themselves*. As he was listening to this presentation, he was thinking, *These people are missing half of the equation*. It reminded Marshall of the great speech by John F. Kennedy: "Ask not what your country can do for you. Ask what you can do for your country." The way they were thinking about employee engagement was exactly the opposite of the Kennedy speech. It was all about what somebody would do for you and how you can't do anything for yourself.

That realization was a turning point. It became clear that engagement—real, lasting engagement—doesn't just come from external rewards or programs. It comes from within. It's a choice. Think about this: Say two flight attendants work for the same airline, wear the same uniform, and earn the same salary. One of them is positive, motivated, upbeat, and enthusiastic. The other one is negative, bitter, angry, and cynical. They're on the same three-hour flight. Who is the real loser in that three-hour flight with that negative, bitter, and angry flight attendant? It's not the passengers. After about five minutes, the passengers couldn't care less about the flight attendant. Who's the real loser for three hours? *The flight attendant with the attitude problem*. Why? Because they choose to allow their negative attitude to impact their professional and personal life, missing out on the potential happiness and satisfaction that can come from engaging positively with their work and the people around them.

The difference isn't in in the circumstances. Same pay, same uniform, same employee engagement program. What's the difference? Not what's on the outside. The difference is what's on the inside—it's the mindset. It's in the choices that person makes every day about how to show up. Choices that they can change and control if they'd just learn to take responsibility.

What Are Daily Questions?

The Daily Questions process is a simple tool for self-accountability. Every day, you ask yourself a set of questions about behaviors you want to improve. Each question begins with, "Did I do my best to . . . ?" This wording is intentional—it focuses on effort, not outcomes.

The six specific questions we recommend starting with are designed to encourage active engagement with your goals and personal development:

1. ***"Did I do my best to set clear goals?"*** Setting clear goals is fundamental to achieving success. This question prompts you to focus on whether you have defined what you want to accomplish clearly enough to guide your actions.
2. ***"Did I do my best to make progress toward goal achievement?"*** Progress is a key motivator and indicator of success. This question ensures that you are actively working toward your goals every day.
3. ***"Did I do my best to find meaning?"*** Finding meaning in what you do can lead to greater satisfaction and motivation. This question encourages you to reflect on the purpose behind your actions.
4. ***"Did I do my best to be happy?"*** Happiness is an important aspect of overall well-being. This question reminds you to prioritize your happiness and take steps to foster it daily.
5. ***"Did I do my best to build positive relationships?"*** Positive relationships are crucial for personal and professional success. This question helps you focus on the effort you put into nurturing and maintaining healthy relationships.

6. ***"Did I do my best to be fully engaged?"*** Being fully engaged means being present and committed to whatever you are doing. This question challenges you to reflect on your level of engagement and how it impacts your performance and satisfaction.

These questions are designed to help you take control of your behavior and become the person you want to be by actively trying to improve in areas that are important to you.

This focus on asking better questions also echoes the work of our friend Michael Bungay Stanier, author of *The Coaching Habit.** Michael's built an entire approach to leadership and behavior change around the idea that simple, well-timed questions can spark big shifts. One of his go-to questions—"What's the real challenge here for you?"—has helped thousands of people slow down, reflect, and make more intentional choices. His message is the same as ours: You don't need complex systems or perfect answers to grow. You just need the right questions and the willingness to keep asking them.

Developing Your Own Daily Questions

Developing your own set of Daily Questions is one of the most powerful tools you can use to increase focus on what really matters in your life. When you create questions that are tied to your personal values, goals, and priorities, you're essentially holding yourself accountable for the things that are most important to *you*. It's like a built-in system for making sure you're living intentionally and making progress where it counts.

---

* Bungay Stanier, Michael. *The Coaching Habit: Say Less, Ask More & Change the Way You Lead Forever*. Page Two, 2016.

For example, if you're trying to improve your health, you might ask, "Did I do my best to exercise today?" or "Did I do my best to make healthy eating choices?" We've even had people ask, "Did I do my best to forgive my parents today?" "Did I do my best not to make angry comments?" and "Did I do my best to delegate effectively and avoid micromanaging?"

Now, here's what happens when you ask yourself these questions every day—you're forced to take a hard look at how well you're doing in those areas. It's structured reflection, and it can be a real game changer. You become more self-aware, you grow, and you start to see where you can improve. Plus, that daily feedback? It's immediate, and it's motivating. It helps you make small, consistent improvements, which add up over time. It's about owning what you *can* do. When you focus on effort—as opposed to outcomes—you're empowering yourself to make positive changes, no matter what's going on around you.

How to Implement Daily Questions

Just like the questions themselves, you can adjust the process you use to answer them. It should still have a few basic components. Keep it simple enough that you'll stick to it. Here are the steps you can think about using as a starter set.

1. **Create a Spreadsheet**
   Write your questions in one column, and across the top label the days of the week: Monday, Tuesday, Wednesday, and so on. If you aren't a fan of spreadsheets, any simple grid will do the trick.

2. **Score Yourself**

   Each evening, answer each question with a number. For yes-or-no questions, use 1 for yes and 0 for no. For other questions, rate yourself on a scale from 1 to 10.

3. **Reflect**

   At the end of the week, look at your scores. You'll quickly see where you're making progress and where you're falling short.

4. **Stay Accountable**

   If possible, have someone hold you accountable. Marshall has someone call him on the phone every day. Every day they listen to him, read questions he's written for himself, and record the answers. One time somebody asked Marshall, "Why do you do this? Don't you know the theory about how to change behavior?" Marshall's answer was, "I was ranked the number one leadership thinker in the world and the number one executive coach in the world*, and I'm too undisciplined to do this by myself. I need help, and it's okay."

   It's easy to tell yourself you can just be your own accountability partner. It's much harder to actually do it. If you can't, it's better to ask someone you trust to help you stick to the process.

---

* Marshall's theory of behavior change is centered around measurable, positive change in leadership behavior, judged not by the individual themselves, but by their key stakeholders. This approach is encapsulated in my unique coaching process, which is based on a pay-for-results model, and is found in numerous studies conducted by Marshall, an example of which can be found in: Goldsmith, Marshall and Howard Morgan. "Leadership Is a Contact Sport: The 'Follow-up Factor' in Management Development." *Strategy+Business*. August 25, 2004. https://www.strategy-business.com/article/04307.

And that's it! Six questions, four steps. Two minutes a day, costs you nothing, and can help you change almost anything in your life.

Why Daily Questions Work

The Daily Questions process works because it forces us to look at ourselves in the mirror every single day. There's no hiding when you do this. For instance, one really good question is, "How many times did I try to prove I was right today when it wasn't worth it?" Let me tell you, almost no one ever gets a zero on that one. It's not only humbling; it's a reality check. Asking ourselves this question has been incredibly helpful over time because it encourages us to reflect on our interactions and to focus on what truly matters. This question helps us avoid unnecessary arguments and choose our battles wisely. The key isn't suppressing opinions or avoiding conflict altogether. It's recognizing when insisting on being right is not beneficial to the relationship or situation at hand.

Marshall's friend Jim Moore does the Daily Questions process every day, and he'll tell you it saved his life. He means it too. Daily Questions didn't *kind of* save his life. This practice *did* save his life. One of Jim's questions was, "Are you currently updated on your physical exam?" For the first ninety days of this practice, he said no every day. After ninety days, Jim said to himself, "This is embarrassing. I'm failing a test every day, and I wrote the question. Either I get the exam or quit asking the question."

So, Jim got the exam. And what did the doctor say? The doctor said, "You have cancer."

That was years ago, and he's fine now. And the doctor told him, "Had you waited seven more months, you'd be dead." Jim knew he should have gotten a physical exam, but he didn't do it for ninety days. Asking himself about that on a daily basis was the only thing that got him into his doctor's office. When you hold the mirror to your face every day, you can't hide.

That's why this process works—forget magic or inspiration. The real issue is staring yourself in the face every day and owning your behavior. There's no passing the buck here. The key isn't some preformulated program or your boss or anyone else. They key is you. Just you. You can't fake it with these questions, and that's what makes them truly powerful. They make you take action. Even when it's hard. Even when it's uncomfortable because you feel shame and embarrassment at not having been able to change your own behavior yet. Because honestly, when you ask yourself the same question over and over and don't like the answer, eventually you'll either change or stop asking. And if you stick with it, you get better—because you're the one doing the work.

The Role of Active Questions

Marshall's daughter Kelly—who's not only brilliant but also a fantastic researcher and professor—introduced the concept of active questions to Marshall, and it completely changed the way we think about improvement. Kelly's research on employee engagement revealed a critical flaw: Most engagement surveys rely on passive questions. Things like, "Do you have clear goals?" "Do you have a best friend at work?" "Is your work meaningful?"

Here's the problem: When people answer no to passive questions like these, they tend to blame external factors. "It's the company's fault." "My manager didn't give me clear goals." Sound familiar?

Kelly taught Marshall the power of active questions, which begin with wording like, "Did I do my best to . . . ?" This simple shift is powerful because it's hard to blame others when you're asking yourself about your own efforts.

In a sense, "Did I do my best to . . . ?" is the hardest question you can test yourself on every day. Why is it hard? You can't blame the person who wrote the question. You know it's important. All you have to do to get on the scoreboard is *try*. You don't even have to succeed. You just have to try. Why is that so hard to ask yourself every day? Who's responsible? That would be you. Just you.

Active questions put the ball in your court. They make you focus on what you can control—your effort, your actions, your choices. The key isn't waiting for someone else to step up; the key is you stepping up. Kelly showed how powerful this shift can be. Her research has proven that changing how you frame your questions really works. She ran studies with thousands of people, asking them to *ask themselves* active questions like, "Did I do my best to find meaning?" and "Did I do my best to build positive relationships?" The results were incredible. People who asked themselves these questions every day saw real improvement—not because the world around them changed but because they changed themselves from within.

It's a simple shift, and it makes you look in the mirror and ask, "Am I putting in the effort to get better?" And honestly, when you do this every day, the answer starts to get better and better.

The Science Behind Daily Questions

Marshall has conducted research with more than 2,500 participants who used the Daily Questions process, and the results have been nothing short of remarkable. Of the seventy-nine studies, 37 percent of the participants said, "I improved at everything. I'm happier. My life is more meaningful. I'm better at everything." 65 percent told Marshall, "I improved on at least four out of the six questions." 89 percent said, "I improved on one question." About 11 percent reported no change, and 0.4 percent said the Daily Questions process made things worse for them.

Let's go back to one of those results for a moment. Nearly 90 percent of participants said they improved in at least one key area, that they changed themselves through one of their Daily Questions. This shows that, no matter where you're starting from, this process can help you get better. And here's the best part: It doesn't cost a thing. You don't need expensive tools, fancy software, or endless hours of your time. All it takes is two minutes a day and a willingness to hold up that mirror to yourself and be honest.

Why does it work so well? Because it forces us to focus on the one thing we can control: ourselves. The Daily Questions process gets you to ask yourself, "Did I do my best?" Whether it's being a better listener, staying engaged, or making progress on a specific goal, it shifts the focus from excuses to accountability. What's so great is how universal it is. It doesn't matter if you're a CEO, a teacher, a police officer, or a stay-at-home parent—this process works for everyone. It trains you to value progress, not perfection. By tracking your efforts daily, you create a system that keeps you honest and moving forward.

We've seen this process change lives in ways that are both profound and practical. People have shared how these small, consistent actions helped them turn around relationships, improve their health, and find more happiness in their day-to-day lives. And it's not just the research that proves it—this approach has been replicated with thousands of people around the world. It works across industries, cultures, and roles because it taps into something universal: the power of consistent effort. If you're willing to commit to this simple process, it's amazing what you can achieve.

Why Effort Matters More Than Outcomes

Here's why this matters so much. We spend so much of our lives worrying about results—sales numbers, career milestones, relationships—that we often lose sight of the only thing we truly control: how we show up each day. Asking, "Did I do my best?" isn't trying to get at perfection; it's trying to get at accountability and staying aligned with your values. For us, this practice acts as a personal compass. Whether it's coaching a top executive, writing a book, or simply being present with family, this simple question keeps us grounded and honest with ourselves.

Think of it this way: Life will throw curveballs. Sometimes your best efforts won't yield the outcomes you hoped for. That's not the point. The point is the effort itself, the discipline to keep trying, to keep learning, and to keep showing up. By consistently asking, "Did I do my best?" you cultivate resilience and self-awareness. Over time, this question becomes more than a daily check-in—it becomes a habit that shapes the way you approach challenges, relationships, and even setbacks. It's a tool for living with intention and integrity through small, actionable steps.

Finally, No More Stupid, Boring Meetings

The practice of asking yourself if you've done your best can transform nearly every aspect of your life, including things you dread—like boring meetings. Imagine you're walking into a long meeting full of pointless PowerPoint slides. You are not looking forward to this meeting. So it's easy to zone out and blame the presenter for being boring. What if, before you go into that meeting, you know you're going to be tested at the end of the meeting on four questions: "Did I do my best to be happy?" "Did I do my best to find meaning?" "Did I do my best to build positive relationships and to be fully engaged?" "What is one thing I could do differently to raise my score on those questions?" By asking those questions, you can't blame the presenter for the meeting. You have only yourself to blame if you didn't make the effort to listen and contribute. You can't control the slides or the agenda. You can control your attitude.

Here's the powerful truth: By focusing on doing your best in these areas, the biggest winner isn't your company, your boss, or even your teammates. It's you. You benefit from the shift in energy, the sense of purpose, and the realization that you have control over how you show up. You don't have to be perfect or pretend to love meetings. Instead, by using active questions to reclaim your ability to change, you can improve how you engage with your world.

Daily Questions are all you need to start this transformation. They're a road map for consistent self-improvement, keeping you focused on what you *can* control. They push you to engage, stay accountable, and celebrate small wins. Over time, these seemingly minor efforts build extraordinary results.

Just try it for two weeks. In fact, there's a handy Daily Questions Journal right in the back of this book. Take those questions, write some of your own questions, ask them daily, and watch how your perspective shifts.

Who knows? They might not just improve the way you think about meetings or self-improvement. These questions might just change—or save—your life.

HOW TO DO

Daily Questions

1. The Power of Asking Questions Daily

- Beginning questions with "Did I do my best to..." focuses on effort, not outcomes.
- The practice develops accountability and aligns actions with personal values.

2. Start with Six Key Questions

Did I do my best to:

1. Set clear goals?
2. Make progress toward those goals?
3. Find meaning in my work?
4. Be happy?
5. Build positive relationships?
6. Stay fully engaged?

3. Create a System for Tracking

Use a spreadsheet or grid to track your daily performance.

Rate each question (e.g., 1–10 or yes/no) and reflect on trends weekly.

4. Leverage Feedback and Accountability

Partner with someone you trust for external accountability.

Engage with a coach to help you stay on track.

5. Focus on Progress, Not Perfection

Acknowledge small wins and incremental improvements.

Embrace effort as the primary metric of success.

6. Make It a Daily Habit

Commit to consistent self-reflection to stay aligned with goals.

Recognize Daily Questions as a tool for sustained growth and resilience.

CHAPTER 5

The Obstacles to Daily Practice

Let's talk about what gets in the way of daily practice. As simple as this practice is, there are three main obstacles that can derail even the most well-intentioned efforts: distraction, planner bias, and what Marshall calls the Great Western Disease—the "I'll be happy when . . ." mindset. If we can overcome these barriers, daily reflection helps us become the people we want to be while also strengthening our intrinsic motivation and sense of purpose.

Obstacle 1: Distraction—The Perfect Storm

Distraction is something that affects every single one of us. We live in what we call the "perfect storm" of distraction. Emails, texts, social media, notifications—it's endless, isn't it? Have you ever gone online to look up something simple like the weather, and three hours later you're watching videos about how to train your cat to fetch the paper? Be honest now. We know; we've been there! That's what we call the "monkey mind."

Our monkey mind is always swinging through the trees, jumping from one branch to another. Now, imagine the internet as caffeine for that monkey. Click, click, click—it's jumping all over the place! The internet doesn't just entertain us; it hijacks our focus. Before you know it, whatever you were supposed to do—maybe reflecting on your goals or answering your Daily Questions—is buried under a pile of digital distractions.

And it's not just the internet. It's on-demand TV, video games, multitasking, and those endless notifications pinging at us from our devices. Marshall wrote an article about this twenty years ago. In it, he predicted that media addiction would eventually impact us all. Unfortunately, Marshall was right. Look around, and you'll see the damage: 51 percent of kids spend more than four hours a day on social media.* That's not just a distraction—it's like a disease. We're addicted to the dopamine we get from our devices. Now, do you worry about this? You should, because distraction both wastes time *and* derails our ability to focus on what matters. It takes us away from reflection, from alignment with our goals, and ultimately from living the life we want.

And if all this media noise weren't enough, let's talk about what we call the "high probability of low-probability distractions." What does that mean? Well, it means life is unpredictable. You don't plan for your computer to crash, your car to get a flat tire, or your kid to come home sick from school. These are the low-probability events we rarely see coming but which also have a high probability of happening at some point throughout our lives. When Marshall coaches CEOs, one of the first things he tells them is, "We're going to work together for eighteen months, and during that time, we guarantee you'll have a crisis." They always

---

* "Teens Spend Average of 4.8 Hours on Social Media Per Day," Gallup, August 17, 2023, https://news.gallup.com/poll/512576/teens-spend-average-hours-social-media-per-day.aspx.

ask, "What kind of crisis?" And the answer is, "Who knows?" It could be a health issue, a merger, a market collapse, or a personal tragedy. Trust us; it'll happen. So on top of the nonstop stream of little interruptions, most of us will get derailed by the occasional full-blown crisis.

Distraction doesn't just waste time—it robs you of your ability to reflect. And reflection is what makes Daily Questions so powerful. Without that quiet moment to ask, "Did I do my best to . . . ?" you miss the chance to course correct. It's like driving without a destination in mind—you might eventually get somewhere, but will it be where you wanted to go? For example, when Marshall first started using Daily Questions with clients, he quickly realized how easy it was to let distractions win. Leaders would have every intention of sitting down to answer questions. Then something would always come up: an urgent email, a phone call, or even just the temptation to scroll through social media. Sound familiar?

So what's the solution? Here's what works: structure and intention. That means having someone call you every single day to ask you your Daily Questions. Marshall and I do this ourselves. Why? Because we know ourselves. If we didn't have that accountability, distraction would win. Forget willpower; what's really important is setting up systems that keep us on track. We know it's hard! Life is noisy, and distractions are everywhere. Having that structure—a person who calls you, listens to your answers, and holds you accountable—makes all the difference.

For you, it might look different. Maybe it's setting a daily reminder on your phone or having a trusted friend check in with you. The method doesn't matter as much as the intention behind it. The goal is to create a system that pulls you out of the storm of distractions and back into focus.

Here's a secret: It's never been about being strong enough to resist distractions. It's always been about being smart enough to design an environment where you don't have to.

Think about it. If your goal is to eat healthier, then don't stock your pantry with junk food and rely on willpower to avoid it. Instead, create a system—maybe by meal prepping or keeping healthy snacks on hand—that sets you up for success.

The same goes for fighting distractions. Don't try to white-knuckle your way through the noise. Instead, build structures that make it easier to focus. For us, it's that daily call. For you, it might be something as simple as turning off notifications during your reflection time or dedicating a specific spot in your home to quiet thinking.

When you take control of distractions, you take control of your life. Suddenly, those moments of reflection become special. They become the time when you reconnect with your values, your goals, and the person you want to be. So, let's make a pact, right here, right now. Let's stop letting distractions dictate our days. Instead, let's build systems that keep us grounded. Let's reclaim our focus and set ourselves up for success with our Daily Questions. We don't have to be perfect. That's not the point. It's about showing up, every day, with intention.

Obstacle 2: Planner Bias—The Gap Between Knowing and Doing

Here's something that trips up almost everyone, from CEOs to aspiring leaders. It's called planner bias, and it's sneaky. Planner bias is this illusion we all have that the version of you making the plan is the same as the version of you who will execute it. Here's the issue: Those two versions of you live in completely different worlds.

Picture this. It's early in the morning, and planner-you is feeling great. You're fresh, full of optimism, and ready to take on the day. "I'll eat a healthy salad for lunch," planner-you says. "I'll hit the gym after work. Maybe I'll even meditate tonight!" Now fast-forward to noon. Doer-you is hungry. You're staring at a greasy burger that smells amazing, and that healthy salad is starting to sound like rabbit food. Suddenly, planner-you's great ideas don't seem so great anymore, do they?

It's the same story in so many parts of life. Planner-you says, "I'll answer our Daily Questions tonight. No problem." Then when tonight rolls around, doer-you is tired, distracted, and scrolling through social media instead. "I'll do it later," you tell yourself. The problem with that is later almost never comes.

We've told you about the research with Daily Questions. Almost 90 percent of people who stuck to this practice saw real progress. Only 11 percent reported no change, and just 0.4 percent said they got worse. So if the process works so well, why doesn't everyone do it? It's not because people are lazy, weak, or bad. It's because we're all busy, and in today's world, it's hard to motivate ourselves.

We see this all the time. People understand what they need to do. They can even explain it back to us in detail: "I need to reflect daily. I need to align my actions with my goals." They *know* it. Yet when it comes time to actually do it, they hesitate. It's not because they're unwilling—it's because their planner-self is not the same as their doer-self.

Let's break this down. Planner-you is optimistic. Planner-you is excited about the possibilities. The gap between planner-you and doer-you is one of the biggest reasons people struggle with Daily Questions—or any self-improvement process, for that matter. Planner-you has all the motivation in the world. Doer-you is tired, hungry, stressed, or distracted. Planner-you sees a future of possibilities. Doer-you is just trying to get through the next hour.

Here's a classic example. When it came out, Marshall's book *What Got You Here Won't Get You There* was the number one best-selling business book in the United States. He was thrilled. Do you know what outsold that book ten times over? The number one best-selling *diet book*. Americans keep buying diet books, and guess what? The books aren't working. If buying diet books made you thin, we'd be the skinniest people in the history of the world! No one loses weight just buying a diet book. The planner-you who buys the book isn't the same as the doer-you who has to resist the chocolate cake.

So how do you close this gap? You don't rely on willpower. Willpower is a myth—it's a short-term burst of energy that fizzles out when you need it most. Instead, you rely on structure. Like we do. Why? Because we know that without that structure, we'll let planner-us off the hook. We'll tell ourselves, "I'll do it tomorrow." And tomorrow turns into never. When you make Daily Questions part of a routine—like brushing your teeth or taking a shower—you eliminate the need for motivation. It just becomes what you do. And when you stick with it, you start to see real results.

Progress doesn't happen all at once. Though the gap between knowing and doing may be real, it's not insurmountable. With the right structure, you can bridge that gap and start living the life planner-you always envisioned. So, the next time planner-you makes a promise, give doer-you the tools to follow through. Set yourself up for success. And remember: Willpower won't cut it. All of us need structure.

Obstacle 3: The Great Western Disease—"I'll Be Happy When . . ."

Let's talk about one of the most common traps we all fall into—it's what we call the Great Western Disease: our tendency to postpone our happiness until we've reached some arbitrary goal or mile-marker. The main symptom of this disease is the phrase, "I'll be happy when . . ." You've probably said it to yourself a hundred times. "I'll be happy when I get that promotion." "I'll be happy when I lose ten pounds." "I'll be happy when my boss finally notices all my hard work." Sound familiar? Here's the catch: "When" never comes. Or if it does, it's temporary. You get the promotion, and for a moment it feels fantastic. Then what happens? You start obsessing about the next big thing—your new responsibilities, a bigger goal, or a tougher challenge. The cycle never ends. The finish line keeps moving further and further away, and before you know it, you're chasing a mirage.

Now, don't get us wrong. Ambition is a wonderful thing. Setting goals and striving to achieve them is part of what makes life exciting.

> *That said, when your happiness is tied to a future event—when you're outsourcing your own joy to some external milestone—you're setting yourself up for disappointment. Why? Because the truth is that happiness doesn't live in the future. It lives right here, right now.*

Here's something we've learned over the years. We all have this incredible ability to lie to ourselves. One of the biggest delusions we cling to is the belief that we have the wisdom and courage to objectively evaluate our own behavior. Well, we don't. Remember the little experiment we told you about? We asked more than eighty thousand people to rank themselves relative to their professional peers. Guess what we found? About 70 percent of people believe they're in the top 10 percent. Think about that for a second—70 percent of people think they're in the top 10 percent! Another 82 percent think they're in the top 20 percent. And 98.5 percent of people are absolutely convinced they're above average. Now, think about this: How is that even possible? It's not. What we've learned is that successful people are often the most delusional. The more successful we become, the more likely we are to think, "We've got this all figured out." Have you ever noticed how, when you get promoted, suddenly your jokes get funnier? Your comments seem more profound? People tell you, "Wow, you have great ideas!" It's all part of the illusion. Even with all this success, even with all these accolades, we still fall into the trap of "I'll be happy when . . ."

Marshall had a client once—a brilliant guy. By every external measure, he was a huge success. He had the title, the corner office, the financial security, you name it. Then one day he came to Marshall and said, "I just don't feel fulfilled. What's wrong with me?" Marshall asked him if he was happy. He said, "You know, it never occurred to me to try to be happy." He started working on Daily Questions and picked a simple one: "Did I do my best to enjoy the moment today?" At first, he struggled with it. He was so used to chasing the next big thing that he didn't know how to appreciate the present. And over time something remarkable happened. He started noticing the little things—a great conversation with a colleague, a moment of gratitude with his family, even the satisfaction of crossing something off his to-do list. What he realized—and what we want you to realize—is that happiness isn't something you achieve later. It's something you create now.

Let's dig a little deeper. The Great Western Disease doesn't just rob you of happiness—it keeps you stuck. It's the ultimate delay tactic. Think about it. How often do we say, "I'll start my new exercise routine after this project is done," or "I'll spend more time with my family once I get through this busy season at work"? The problem is, there's always another project, another busy season, another excuse. And while you're waiting for the perfect moment, life keeps moving. Before you know it, years have gone by, and you're still waiting for "when" to come. Here's something we've learned from coaching some of the most successful people in the world: They all need help. And guess what? That's okay. Top athletes have coaches. Movie stars have personal trainers. They don't rely on willpower alone—they build systems that keep them on track. The same goes for happiness. You don't just wake up one day and say, "I'm happy now." You create habits and structures that help you find joy in the present moment.

This is where Daily Questions come in. Instead of saying, "I'll be happy when . . . ," you ask yourself, "Did I do my best to be happy today?" It's a subtle and profound shift. When you start focusing on what you can do right now, you take control of your happiness. You stop waiting for external validation and start finding joy in the process. Maybe you didn't hit every goal today. The question is: Did you make an effort? Did you try? That's what matters.

One of the most important lessons we've learned—and one that we hope will stick with you—is that it's okay to need help. It's okay to need structure. When you accept that, life gets a whole lot better. So the next time you catch yourself saying, "I'll be happy when . . . ," stop and ask yourself: "What can I do to be happy *right now*?" It might be something small—a kind word to a friend, a moment of gratitude, or even just pausing to take a deep breath. If you focus on it with real intention, it can have a profound impact on you.

Happiness isn't out there waiting for you. It's right here, right now. And the sooner you let go of the Great Western Disease, the sooner you'll realize that everything you need to be happy is already within your reach.

We've got to stop chasing a finish line that keeps moving and start appreciating the journey. So don't wait for "when." Start today. Ask yourself, "Did I do my best to enjoy the moment?"

Because the only moment you truly have is this one, right here, right now.

DAILY QUESTIONS AND

Overcoming Obstacles

1. Acknowledge Distraction as a Major Obstacle

Recognize the "perfect storm" of digital distractions and unexpected crises.

Understand that distractions rob us of focus and reflection.

2. Combat Distraction with Structure and Intention

Build systems to counter distractions, such as accountability partners or turning off phones. Focus on creating an environment that minimizes the temptation to become distracted.

3. Bridge the Gap Between Planning and Doing

- ☑ Identify the difference between planner-you (optimistic) and doer-you (realistic).
- ☑ Create structures that eliminate reliance on willpower, like integrating daily habits.

4. Overcome the Great Western Disease: "I'll Be Happy When..."

Stop postponing happiness for future achievements.

Recognize that happiness comes from appreciating the present moment.

☺ ☺ ☺ ☺ ☺ ☺ ☺

5. Adopt Daily Questions to Foster Present-Focused Growth

- Ask intentional questions like, "Did I do my best to enjoy the moment today?"
- Use these questions to align actions with goals and values in the now.

6. Embrace Progress Over Perfection

Focus on effort, not outcomes, to create sustainable growth and happiness.

Understand that true happiness and fulfillment come from consistent, intentional action.

CHAPTER 6

Measuring What Matters to You

One of the biggest traps we face today is what we call "Comparison Culture." It's everywhere—on social media, at work, even in our personal lives. We're constantly comparing ourselves to others, measuring our worth against the highlight reels of friends, colleagues, and megastars. Here's the truth: You can't win at someone else's game. The only way to truly grow and succeed is to measure what matters to *you*.

Why? Because what gets measured gets managed, as Peter Drucker used to say. When you measure what matters to you—whether it's being a better listener, staying true to your values, or simply taking small steps toward a goal—you're creating a road map for meaningful progress. This is about reclaiming control over how you measure success. By focusing on your own growth and values, you can escape the comparison trap and create a life that's truly fulfilling. You'll be amazed at what happens when you start measuring what truly matters.

The Antidote to Success Culture and Comparison Culture

A while back, Marshall and his daughter Kelly engaged with more than one hundred young professionals from across the globe.* These future leaders were ambitious, talented, and driven, and as Marshall and Kelly listened to their concerns, two major societal forces emerged as recurring themes.

Success Culture

The first trend they call "Success Culture." Over the past few decades, we've seen a monumental shift in how society glorifies elite achievement. A select few—the megastars of their fields—are now earning levels of recognition and wealth that were unthinkable for their predecessors. CEOs, founders, entertainers, athletes, and influencers today can make hundreds, even thousands, of times more than those in comparable positions from previous generations. And they're doing it younger and younger, creating an aura of enviable perfection around their accomplishments.

Success Culture creates unrealistic standards beyond just career. The constant visibility of megastars' personal lives—exotic vacations, peak fitness, thriving relationships—makes us feel small and dull. The message we take away? Just being good at your job isn't enough anymore. You've got to be so extraordinary that the whole world sits up and takes notice. Anything less? Well, it just feels like you're not cutting it.

---

* Marshall Goldsmith and Kelly Goldsmith, "Helping People Achieve Their Goals," Marshall Goldsmith, March 31, 2014, https://marshallgoldsmith.com/articles/helping-people-achieve-their-goals/.

It's like we're all drinking a cocktail of inspiration and intimidation. And it's a potent mix. It leaves a lot of folks feeling frustrated and inadequate. And it's not just the young professionals feeling this way. Success Culture is getting to people of all ages and all walks of life.

In light of this, it's critical for anyone struggling with these feelings to push back against the negative aspects of Success Culture. This starts with changing the story we're telling ourselves. Rather than focusing on external markers like income, titles, or social media clout, we should emphasize intrinsic milestones: meaningful contributions, personal growth, and the fulfillment that comes from aligning our work with our values.

This is where Daily Questions can be a game changer. They help you measure your success by your own yardstick, not someone else's. Because at the end of the day, that's what really counts. Success isn't about keeping up with the latest celebrity. It's about being true to yourself and your own definition of a life well lived.

Comparison Culture

Right alongside Success Culture is its equally toxic relative, Comparison Culture. With social media's ever-present magnifying glass, we can now peer into the lives of hyper-successful megastars *and* our own classmates, colleagues, and acquaintances. It's often the achievements of people within our own circles that brings on Comparison Culture. One person's vacation photos or career successes may become benchmarks for someone else's personal success. You got a promotion? Great! Your college roommate just started their own company. You finally ran that 5K? Wonderful! Your neighbor just completed an Ironman. It's getting harder and harder to feel good about our own progress when we're constantly bombarded with everyone else's successes.

And Comparison Culture isn't just about seeing how you measure up to your friends or coworkers anymore; it's a full-blown global phenomenon where everyone is stacked up against the world's most visible and elite performers. Whether it's tech moguls, top athletes, social media influencers, or CEOs, we are bombarded with stories of extraordinary success. These stories are inspiring for some, sure, though for many they create a dangerous sense of inadequacy.

When Marshall and his daughter spoke to the young professionals, it was striking how deeply this dynamic was affecting young people. Social media was designed for connection, but it's turned into a platform that *amplifies comparison*. Marshall and Kelly heard stories of how simply scrolling on their phones could turn from a harmless habit into a source of anxiety in an instant. Seeing others' accomplishments posted on social media with tons of likes and supportive comments was making them question their own paths. "Why am I not there yet?" "What am I doing wrong?" It's like a broken record playing in their heads. Even for those who are objectively successful, these images make them think they're somehow falling short.

One young leader shared that despite receiving a significant promotion and pay raise, they felt deflated after seeing a former classmate announce their startup had just secured millions in funding. Another one mentioned how they felt that even with an MBA and earning a six-figure salary in their early thirties, they were somehow "behind" because they hadn't yet founded a tech unicorn or been on the cover of a magazine.

Can you believe that? A six-figure salary in your early thirties, and you're feeling behind? That's what Success Culture is doing to us.

The relentless exposure to others' curated lives makes it tougher than ever to celebrate personal milestones. Instead of focusing on their own progress, these accomplished people are stuck chasing an ever-moving target set by the achievements of others.

The broader implications of Comparison Culture are downright worrisome. Research shows that the constant visibility of others' successes is driving up rates of anxiety, depression, and dissatisfaction throughout entire societies. Take a place like Japan. The pressure to excel is off the charts. Here's a country that's got it all—education, economic power, you name it. But you know what else they've got? Alarmingly high rates of mental health issues and suicide among their young people. This isn't a cultural issue—it's a human one, magnified by the universal accessibility of social media. In Japan, it's amplifying the already intense societal pressures to be perfect in school, at work, and even in how people look.

It's a tough situation, no doubt about it. But recognizing the problem is the first step to fixing it. We need to start having some serious conversations about how we're measuring success and what it's doing to our mental health.

The Toll on Mental Health, Well-Being, and Self-Perception

Now, let's talk about the consequences of combining Success Culture and Comparison Culture. The constant exposure to the lives of the ultra-successful and the accomplishments of peers has led to a mental health crisis for many, many people.

Let's consider another country: South Korea—a textbook example of extraordinary economic success combined with relentless comparison. Over the past few decades, South Korea has transformed itself from one of the poorest countries in the world to one of the richest and most educated. This success has come at a big price. The rates of anxiety, depression, loneliness, and suicide? They're through the roof, especially among young people. It's like a full-blown mental health crisis driven by an intense pressure to succeed and constant comparison.

South Korea's struggles illustrate how Comparison Culture warps self-perception. The country leads the world in cosmetic surgery, and not because their people aren't already beautiful. And social media? It's like pouring gasoline on the fire, showing all these perfectly posted images that drum up feelings of inadequacy.

And it doesn't stop there. This comparison game is messing with every aspect of life. Take the birth rate globally, for example. It's now the lowest in history. Why? Maybe something that's contributing to it in developed countries like South Korea is that people are feeling so overwhelmed and inadequate that they're putting off starting families. It's like we're caught in this never-ending race to succeed, to look perfect, to meet these sky-high benchmarks. And in the process, we're losing sight of what really matters: personal fulfillment, building families, enjoying life.

What truly stands out is how deeply these dynamics affect even the most accomplished individuals, regardless of where they live. When Marshall and Kelly interviewed the group of young professionals, it was striking how often top earners—those in the top 1 percent of their age group—described feeling undervalued and unfulfilled. These are individuals with high six-figure salaries, prestigious degrees, and impressive titles, yet they spoke about their careers with words like "disappointing" and "frustrating." Why? Because their accomplishments, remarkable as they are, pale in comparison to the extraordinary lives they see others projecting. This is what happens when Comparison Culture goes into overdrive.

This phenomenon distorts self-perception, turning victories into disappointments. Instead of celebrating their achievements—earning an MBA, securing a dream job, or making significant career strides—people only see *what they haven't yet achieved* relative to someone else. This relentless self-comparison creates a gap between how they perceive themselves and the reality of their success.

Combating the Comparison Trap

One practical way to combat this mindset is through Daily Questions, which redirect focus from external validation to internal fulfillment. Since Daily Questions are self-reflective questions you ask yourself every day, they can help realign your actions with what truly matters. Questions like, "Did I do my best to make progress toward my goals today?" or "Did I act in a way that reflects my values?" help people focus on their own journey and recognize their own wins. The key here is consistency. By revisiting these questions daily, people can shift their attention from unattainable external benchmarks to the tangible progress they're making in their own lives. And again, effort matters more than outcomes. Effort is what *you* can control.

An executive we coached shared how this practice revolutionized her perspective. Each evening, she asked herself, "Did I recognize the progress I made today, however small?" and "Did I take at least one meaningful step toward my goals?" These Daily

Questions became a mental reset, pulling her attention away from the highlight reels of social media and back to her own efforts and growth. She began to see her own achievements—mentoring a colleague, closing a deal, or learning a new skill—not as small or insignificant. She saw them as meaningful milestones in her personal journey.

Anyone can use this practice to get themselves out of Comparison Culture. The transformation begins with small, consistent actions. Daily Questions provide a practical and accessible tool for reframing success, increasing resilience, and combating the toxic effects of comparison. In a world where highlight reels dominate our lives, asking yourself, "Did I do my best today?" is a simple and powerful step toward a healthier, more grounded outlook on success.

Here's a Story about Sarah and Alex

Sarah is a brilliant managing director at a top investment bank, someone who's really earned her stripes in a tough industry. A few years ago, she was frustrated—though not with her own career. She was frustrated with a younger colleague, Alex, who was spiraling into what we call the "Comparison Culture Trap."

Alex was one of her rising stars. He was sharp, ambitious, and a real workhorse. By all measures, the guy was excelling at life—nearly a seven-figure salary, closing massive deals, and already living the dream at age twenty-eight. Then Sarah noticed something was off. He'd stopped celebrating his wins. Even after closing one of the biggest deals of his career, he seemed deflated, like it wasn't good enough. She said, "I've seen this before, and I can't quite figure out how to help him."

So we asked her, "What's bothering Alex?"

Sarah said, "He's stuck in this cycle of comparing himself to everyone around him—colleagues, classmates, people on Instagram. It's not just the billionaires of the world; it's his old MBA buddy who just got featured in *Forbes*. It's that colleague who got promoted six months ahead of him. He's constantly asking himself, 'Why am I not doing better?' And it's eating away at him."

Sarah continued, "Alex is doing great on paper. At the same time, he feels like he's falling behind because he's measuring himself against a standard that's impossible to reach."

We told her, "This isn't just an Alex problem. This is the Comparison Culture we talk about all the time. Social media, instant communication, all these highlight reels—it's like pouring rocket fuel on insecurity. And the more successful you are, the harder it can hit you. Luckily, we've got a practice that can help him."

Now, Sarah's smart—she knows there's no quick fix for someone who's stuck in a mindset like this. So we introduced her to the idea of Daily Questions and told her they've helped a lot of people we've worked with, including some of the most successful CEOs in the world.

We told her, "Look, Sarah, Alex needs to stop focusing on other people's wins and start focusing on what really matters to him. These Daily Questions—simple, reflective prompts—can help him shift his attention back to his own values and progress. They're not about perfection; they're about consistency."

Sarah loved the idea and decided to tell Alex about it during one of their one-on-one chats. Here's how it went down, as she told us later.

She said to Alex, "Listen, I've been where you are. Early in my career, I couldn't stop comparing myself to the people around me.

Then someone taught me a trick that changed everything. Every night, I ask myself a few questions. 'Did I do my best today to move toward my goals?' 'Did I recognize my progress, no matter how small?' 'Was I the kind of person I want to be?' It helped me focus less on what others are doing and more on making sure I'm doing my best."

At first, Alex thought it sounded stupid. Sarah challenged him to try it for two weeks. "What do you have to lose?" she asked.

Fast-forward a month, and Alex was a different person. He started looking forward to his daily check-in with himself. Instead of scrolling through his social media feed at night, comparing his life to someone else's, he sat down and reflected on his own progress. For the first time in months, he felt proud of his work—and not because someone else validated it. It was because he saw the value himself.

Sarah told us that Alex even started mentoring junior analysts in his new practice. He'd tell them, "Don't worry about what everyone else is doing. Focus on your own game. Measure success by the progress you're making, not by someone else's playbook."

Here's the best part: Sarah said Alex started asking her some of the same reflective questions during their meetings. "What am I doing well?" "Where can I improve?" "How can I make the biggest contribution to our team?" She said it completely changed the way they worked together.

Now, here's the lesson: We all get stuck in the Comparison Culture sometimes. It's human nature. When you focus on what you can control—your own effort, your own growth—you take back the power that comparison steals from you. You don't have to win all the time. You definitely don't have to be more miserable than everybody around you. Doing Daily Questions doesn't take a massive overhaul. It starts with one simple question: "Did I do my best today?" That's all it takes. Small steps, every day.

Additional Practical Strategies

While we don't have all the answers for what leaders and professionals face today because of Comparison Culture, we can offer some practical strategies that we believe can make a difference.

1. **Shift the Focus to Contributions**
   Encourage those around you or your direct reports to take pride in their unique efforts and the positive impact they're making. Instead of measuring success by fame, money, or likes on social media, help them see the value of their work within their organization, community, or the world at large. Many people genuinely want to make a difference—show them how their contributions matter.

2. **Help, Don't Judge**
   Let's face it: Every generation thinks the one after it is "entitled" or "ungrateful." It's an old refrain that's never helped anyone. Instead of criticizing, let's empathize. Understand the unique challenges people are facing in today's hyper-connected, high-pressure world. Building bridges starts with mutual respect and curiosity.

3. **Counter the Obsession with Megastars**
   Within organizations, resist the temptation to idolize the ultra-successful. Celebrate everyday wins. Highlight the value of teamwork, perseverance, and personal growth.

These are the achievements that build long-term, sustainable success—not the fleeting glamour of being a megastar.

The Path to Meaning

Ultimately, combating comparison culture is about shifting the narrative. Instead of measuring success by external markers—titles, salaries, or social media clout—let's focus on personal growth, meaningful contributions, and realistic expectations.

For leaders and would-be leaders, this means understanding the unique challenges the people in our organizations face and helping them navigate a world where comparison is almost unavoidable. By focusing on what really matters—contributions, empathy, and personal growth—we can help everyone around us redefine success on their own terms.

So, here's our challenge to you: How can you help someone in your organization today feel valued for who they are and what they bring to the table? That's the real measure of leadership.

MEASURING WHAT

Matters to You

1. Recognize the Impact of Comparison Culture

Understand how social media and "Success Culture" create unrealistic standards and feelings of inadequacy. Acknowledge the mental health toll, including anxiety and dissatisfaction.

2. Focus on Intrinsic Milestones

Shift attention from external benchmarks (titles, wealth) to personal growth and meaningful contributions.

Emphasize progress and alignment with individual values.

3. Combat Comparison Culture with Daily Questions

Use self-reflective prompts like, "Did I do my best to make progress today?"

Focus on tangible efforts rather than unattainable comparisons.

4. Celebrate Everyday Wins

Highlight small, meaningful achievements instead of idolizing megastars.

Reinforce the value of teamwork, perseverance, and incremental growth.

5. Foster Empathy and Support

Encourage understanding rather than judgment when facing others' challenges.

Help others see the positive impact of their contributions within their communities or organizations.

6. Redefine Success Through Leadership

Lead by example, valuing personal growth and realistic expectations.

Challenge others to appreciate their unique strengths and efforts.

PART III

Tools for Sustained Success

"The best leaders understand that leadership and personal growth are inseparable."

— Marshall Goldsmith

CHAPTER 7

Sustaining Mastery and Growth

Answer this question: How often do you lean on others to help you grow? We're not talking about the occasional bit of advice from a friend—we mean real, consistent support from people who hold you accountable, push you to do your best, and cheer you on along the way. If you're like most people, the answer is probably, "Not enough." And that's okay, because we've all been there. Here's the truth: A strong support system can be the difference between striking out in what you want for yourself or hitting it out of the park in ways you never thought possible.

While personal growth is ultimately your responsibility, it doesn't have to be a solo act. In fact, one of the smartest moves you can make is to surround yourself with people who will help you stay on track. This could be a mentor, an accountability partner, or a coach. Whoever it is, their role is simple: to support you, challenge you, and ensure you follow through on the commitments you've made to yourself.

The Value of Accountability Partners, Coaches, and Mentors

Something we've learned over many years is that accountability partners, coaches, and mentors are absolute game changers when it comes to personal growth. They're the ones who make sure the progress you work so hard to achieve doesn't just fizzle out after a few weeks. They're the ones who stick around and become a part of who you are. Why? Because they're the external forces that keep you disciplined even when your internal motivation starts to wane. We've all been there.

With the Daily Questions process, we always emphasize the importance of having someone to hold you accountable. Sure, you might think, *I can do this on my own.* Here's the truth: Most of us overestimate our ability to stay disciplined. Remember, planner-you and doer-you are not the same person. That's where an accountability partner comes in. This can be anyone—a friend, a coworker, a family member—someone you trust who checks in with you and says, "Hey, how'd you do today?" Simple, yet incredibly powerful.

Then there are professional coaches and mentors. These folks bring something special to the table: experience, perspective, and a little push when you need it. They're the ones who help you see your blind spots, challenge you to think bigger, and encourage you to keep going when you're tempted to stop. It's kind of like having a personal trainer. You know the one—cheering you on to finish that last set when you're ready to quit.

We're social creatures. We thrive on connection, and we tend to perform better when we know someone's rooting for us, watching over us. Whether it's encouragement, recognition, or a bit of friendly competition, that social support is huge. It keeps us motivated and helps us see ourselves more clearly. Sometimes we don't notice our own habits or behaviors. Then an outside perspective can reflect our behaviors back to us in a way that's hard to ignore.

Every top athlete has a coach. Why wouldn't it be the same for leaders at the top of their game? Coaching statistics are underreported because not every leader wants to reveal that they need help, but our experience shows that most of the top performers today have a coach at some point in their careers. It's a competitive disadvantage if you don't.

The bottom line that bears repeating: Having accountability partners, coaches, and mentors isn't just helpful—it's essential for sustaining personal growth. They keep us on track, give us valuable feedback, and remind us why we're doing the work in the first place. And most importantly, they help make sure the changes stick with us for the long haul.

Creating the Environment that Nurtures Sustained Engagement

When we think about mentors and colleagues and their role in our growth, it's like they're the secret sauce that makes everything else click. After all, the best leaders know that they cannot go it alone. They help us create an environment where accountability and engagement are baked into how we live and work every day. Accountability and engagement are a lot like what author Daniel Pink describes as autonomy and purpose in his book *Drive*.* Accountability and autonomy are both about intrinsic motivation

---

* Pink, Daniel H. 2009. *Drive: The Surprising Truth About What Motivates Us*. New York: Riverhead Books.

for growth and success. And engagement and purpose are both about people taking ownership of their actions.

First, let's talk about autonomy. Pink describes autonomy as having control over how you do your work, and mentors and colleagues can play a huge role in this. A great mentor doesn't micromanage or tell you exactly what to do. Instead, they empower you. They ask questions that make you think deeply and encourage you to take ownership of your path. It's the same with supportive colleagues—they challenge you in ways that help you grow and still leave room for you to find your own answers. That autonomy makes you more engaged because you feel invested in the process.

Then there's purpose. Pink explains that purpose is all about connecting what you do to something bigger than yourself. Mentors can help you see the bigger picture, whether it's the impact of your work or the legacy you're building. They're the ones who have the perspective to say, "Here's why what you're doing *matters*." And colleagues? They're often the people who remind you, day in and day out, that you're part of a team. Knowing that your efforts contribute to a shared mission or goal can be a huge motivator. It gives your work meaning and keeps you engaged even when things get tough.

When mentors and colleagues are part of your growth, they create a kind of feedback loop. They hold you accountable—though not in a harsh way. Rather, in a way that says, "I believe in you. Let's keep this going." They celebrate your wins, challenge you when you're falling behind, and help you course correct when you veer off track. That sense of connection is what sustains you when your internal drive starts to peter out.

Like Pink's principles of autonomy and purpose, mentors and colleagues provide the structure and support that nurture accountability and engagement. They make sure you're not just growing for the sake of it—you're growing in ways that matter, ways that stick. And that's how real, lasting change happens.

Setting Up Your Network of Support

When it comes to staying on track with Daily Questions, having a solid network of support can make all the difference. You don't have to do this alone—in fact, you shouldn't. Building a support system that reinforces accountability and self-improvement is a good idea.

First, find your initial set of accountability partners—people you trust and respect. These should be individuals who won't shy away from giving you honest feedback and who know your goals and really want to help you succeed. Everyone who plans to use Daily Questions should consider finding at least one accountability partner.

If someone in your life is equally interested in trying the Daily Questions process, you could do some reciprocal coaching. This is where you team up with someone else, coach each other, hold each other accountable, and check in regularly. It's like having a gym buddy for personal growth—and it works because you're both invested.

Then there's mastermind groups. These are small groups of like-minded folks who come together to talk about their goals, challenges, and wins. The shared wisdom and support of the group can be incredibly motivating, not to mention inspiring.

Although your network of support definitely needs to include other people, it can also include tools that you use on your own. If you're into tech, you can use apps or online tools to track your progress and share it with your accountability partners. Seeing your progress visually can be a real boost, and it keeps everyone in the loop.

One thing we can't stress enough is to schedule regular check-ins. Whether it's a call, a meeting, or even a quick text, consistency is everything. It doesn't matter if your accountability partner is your next-door neighbor or a professional coach; check-ins are a must. Knowing you've got that regular touchpoint helps you stay committed.

Here's something else to try for real accountability: Share your commitment publicly. Maybe it's on social media, in your team meeting, or even just with your family. When you tell others about your goals, it creates a sense of responsibility. You're less likely to slack off if you know people are watching.

A Professional Coach Can Help

And finally, consider hiring a professional coach. A professional coach can be a game changer when it comes to sticking with your Daily Questions. We know this from personal experience—it's been a cornerstone of growth.

Why? External accountability. When you know you have to report your progress to someone else—especially someone you're paying—it lights a fire under you. It's one thing to promise yourself you'll follow through. It's another when there's a professional you've hired to help you asking you how you did. You're way more likely to stick with it.

Then there's objective feedback. A coach isn't your friend, your spouse, or your coworker. They don't have emotional baggage or ulterior motives. They give you clear, unbiased insights—sometimes the kind you need to hear even if you might not want to.

A skilled coach can also help you refine your Daily Questions to make sure they're laser-focused on your goals and on what's true and meaningful to you. They know what works from their own experience and can tweak your approach so you get better results. And don't overlook the value of encouragement. When you hit a rough patch—and trust us; we all do—a coach is there to remind you why you started. They'll keep you motivated and help you stay on track even when it feels tough.

Perspective is key. Sometimes we get so caught up in the day-to-day grind that we lose sight of the bigger picture. A coach can help you step back and see how your daily efforts fit into your long-term goals. That perspective can be a real lifesaver. Structure is valuable too. A good coach will help you set up a system that works for you. They'll keep things organized and consistent, which makes it far more likely you'll stick with the practice over the long haul. And finally, clarification. Coaches help you get crystal clear on your values. They make sure your Daily Questions align with what truly matters to you, so every effort you make is meaningful.

Even as a coaches ourselves, we value having a coach. Our own coaches have helped us maintain discipline, grow, and keep improving. So if you're serious about making the most of your Daily Questions and your self-improvement journey, hiring a coach might just be one of the best decisions you make.

To put it simply: Growth isn't a straight line. There will be setbacks, detours, and moments when you want to throw in the towel. That's where your support system comes in. Your colleagues, accountability partners, mentors, and coaches will remind you why you started, help you get back on track, and cheer you on when you make progress. Now, we'll leave you with this challenge: Who will you invite into your life? Who will you trust to hold you accountable, push you to be better, and celebrate your growth? Take a moment to think about it—and then take action. Because when it comes to growth, the right support system can make all the difference.

The Role of Mastery and Habits in Sustained Growth

Now that we've covered who can support you, let's talk about mastery. Mastery—that desire to get better at something meaningful—is a big one. What really matters about mastery: It's not something you achieve overnight. It's built, brick by brick, through small, consistent habits. Habits are the building blocks of mastery. Every small step you take strengthens your skills, boosts your confidence, and gives you a sense of competence. Achieving mastery brings about permanence. The way to get there is one hour at a time. And it helps if you learn to enjoy the process.

This is where Daily Questions come in. When you ask yourself something like, "Did I do my best to set clear goals today?" you're not aiming for perfection. You're focusing on the effort. And that's a game changer. Why? Because effort drives progress, and progress—not perfection—is what keeps us motivated. You keep moving closer, and that's where the meaning lies.

Now, let's talk about feedback loops, because they're another big reason Daily Questions work so well. We've mentioned feedback loops a few times already, and now we want to introduce you to some people who take them to a whole new level. Have you ever heard of the Quantified Self Movement? It's this remarkable community of people who track personal data—everything from steps taken to hours slept—all to better understand and improve their lives. One of the big insights from this movement is the power of feedback loops.* When you measure something, you're not just collecting data—you're creating a mirror for your behavior. Here's how it works with Daily Questions. Let's say you ask, "Did I do my best to build positive relationships today?" At the end of the day, you reflect on your actions and give yourself a score. Maybe you reached out to an old friend or listened more attentively to a colleague. That's a win, and seeing it motivates you to keep it up tomorrow. And when you see patterns—like, "Hey, I'm doing a lot better at this than I thought"—that creates momentum. You don't have to be perfect; you just have to see progress.

The Quantified Self people figured this out. They found that even simple metrics can change behavior in profound ways. Tracking your steps makes you walk more. Tracking your sleep makes you prioritize rest. And tracking your Daily Questions? That makes you more intentional about your life. It's all about clarity and focus. You see where you're doing well, where you're slipping, and what adjustments you need to make. It's not blaming yourself that makes a difference; it's learning. Beating ourselves up rarely helps us improve, especially in the long term. One of our favorite things about this process is how it shifts the focus from outcomes to effort. That's huge. You're not asking, "Did I achieve perfect results today?" You're asking, "Did I try?" That simple shift takes the pressure off and creates space for experimentation and growth.

Here's an example. Suppose you're working on strengthening your relationships. You ask, "Did I do my best to connect with

---

* "Quantified self through little fill-in boxes," One Thousand Lightbulbs, May 13, 2020, https://1klb.com/posts/2020/05/13/quantified-self-through-little-fill-in-boxes/.

others today?" Maybe you sent a quick thank-you email to a colleague or took five extra minutes to really listen to a friend. These small actions add up. Over time, they compound into meaningful improvements.

This approach to measuring progress is forgiving, which is what makes it sustainable. Life isn't perfect, and neither are we. That's okay. As long as you're trying, you're winning. The idea of mastery dovetails beautifully with this. You're not trying to "arrive" somewhere; you're trying to get a little better every day. We often remind our clients that the road to mastery usually follows the rule of thirds. One third of the time will feel great. One third will feel just okay. And one third will feel painful and like progress is slow. It's all part of the process—*just keep going.* And that's what makes Daily Questions such a powerful tool for sustained growth. They help you focus on what you can control—your effort—and create a road map for becoming the person you want to be.

When we work with executives, we make sure the feedback process is constructive by enlisting their colleagues. We ask them to commit to four principles:

1. Let go of the past: We can't change what happened last month or last week. Focus on how the individual can improve going forward.
2. Tell the truth: Honest feedback is essential for real growth.
3. Be supportive: Approach feedback with the intention of helping, not criticizing.
4. Commit to improving yourself: Feedback works best when everyone involved is focused on growth.

At the end of the day, the real story isn't reaching some mythical state of perfection; it's striving to be just a little better than you were yesterday. And you know what? The secret to doing that is realizing you don't have to do it alone. When you surround yourself with the right people—mentors, coaches, accountability partners—they help you stay on track even when your motivation dips.

To paraphrase a well-known saying, mastery is a journey, not a destination. It's about showing up consistently, making the effort, and enjoying the process of getting closer to becoming the person you want to be. That's what growth is about too—small steps, steady progress, and a little help from the people who care about us. You can create a life that embraces accountability, improvement, and fulfillment. Let's keep showing up for ourselves—and for one another.

BUILDING SUPPORT

Systems

1. Identify Support Systems

Find accountability partners, coaches, and mentors to sustain progress.

They offer discipline, perspective, and encouragement to fuel growth.

2. Roles of Accountability

Partners, Coaches, and Mentors

- Accountability partners ensure daily check-ins to stay on track.
- Coaches and mentors provide experience, uncover blind spots, and inspire growth.
- Social support motivates and enhances self-awareness.

3. Foster Accountability and Engagement

Coaches help align efforts with larger goals and provide feedback.

Sustain engagement through feedback, goal alignment, and celebrating wins.

4. Build a Support Network

Combine accountability partners, coaches, and groups for consistent progress.

Use tools like apps or meetings to track and review progress.

5. Focus on Mastery and Habits

Prioritize small, consistent efforts over perfection.

Use Daily Questions to align actions with goals and build momentum.

6. Leverage Feedback and Reflection

Use feedback to guide improvement with honesty and support.

Reflect on effort daily with questions like, "Did I do my best today?"

CHAPTER 8

More Strategies for the Future You

We've already given you a number of research-backed strategies and tactics, and here's another one: "Feedforward." Many people are afraid of feedback because they think they'll be berated for past shortcomings. The simple reframe of Feedforward is to share ideas for how a person can be even better in the future. We love the Feedforward concept because it's such a simple idea, and it's incredibly effective for becoming the person you want to be. It's all about focusing on future possibilities and positive change. Feedforward shifts the focus from what's already happened—which you can't change—to what you *can* do going forward. It helps you envision a better version of yourself and concentrate on actionable steps to make it permanent.

Unlike feedback, which often looks at past behaviors and sometimes feels critical or negative, Feedforward is inherently positive and constructive. It encourages you to think, *What can I do differently?* or *How can I grow?* That kind of future-focused thinking is empowering. It reinforces the belief that you're capable of change and growth no matter where you're starting from.

What's great about this approach is how it helps create a vision for your future self and gets you to take concrete steps to make that vision a reality. It's also a good way to build a growth mindset. When you embrace Feedforward, you're saying to yourself, *I can develop new skills. I can adapt. I can improve.* And when you learn from others' insights and ideas, you open up even more possibilities for growth. None of us can do this alone. And we can't be truly self-aware without the observations and inputs of others. This process allows you to tap into the brilliance of people who are all around you.

When you make Feedforward a regular practice, you create a positive cycle. It focuses on your potential, not your limitations, and that can be a game changer. It builds confidence, resilience, and momentum—everything you need to pursue your goals and become the person you aspire to be.

Key Principles of Feedforward

The process for Feedforward involves a positive, future-focused approach to personal and professional development. It's a method we've used both individually with clients and in large groups. The essence of Feedforward is to engage in two things: learning as much as you can and helping as much as you can. It's about creating an environment where everyone is focused on giving and receiving constructive suggestions for the future rather than dwelling on past mistakes.

There are two key rules that make Feedforward work so well:

- **First, we don't talk about the past.** When you stick to what someone *can* do, rather than what they *didn't* do, you avoid all the defensiveness and negativity that usually comes with feedback. It keeps the energy positive, forward-looking, and focused on improvement. No one wants to be reminded of their mistakes—they want to hear how they can be even better.
- **Second, there's no critique of ideas.** If someone gives you a suggestion, the only thing you say is, "Thank you." That's it! Saying these two words—without adding anything else—goes a long way. It acknowledges the feedback as a gift without coming across as defensive or dismissive. Whether the feedback is good or bad, showing gratitude shifts the focus to how it can help you improve moving forward. This simple habit creates a positive environment where people feel heard and valued, making open communication and learning a natural part of the process. Plus, it strengthens relationships by showing humility and respect for different perspectives. As Marshall always says, focus on the future you can change, not the past you can't.

These two principles are game changers. They make the process enjoyable and productive because the focus isn't on blame; it's on building a better future.

Treat Suggestions as Gifts

As we begin to use Feedforward in our lives, one of the simplest and most powerful things we can do to foster a positive, collaborative environment is to treat all suggestions like gifts. Think about it: When someone offers a suggestion, they're giving you a little piece of themself. They've taken the time, put in the thought, and shared something they believe might help. That's a big deal! Even if you don't end up using their idea, acknowledging it with gratitude shows that you respect the effort and care behind it.

Here's why having this mindset makes such a difference.

First, it creates a safe space for honest exchanges. People are much more likely to share their ideas when they know those ideas will be met with appreciation rather than criticism or dismissal. And we all know, nothing shuts down creativity faster than feeling like your input doesn't matter.

Second, it encourages collaboration. When everyone sees their suggestions are genuinely valued, they'll feel more inspired to contribute their own ideas. And when you've got that kind of momentum, the best solutions tend to rise to the surface.

It also builds trust. Taking a moment to say, "Thank you," for a suggestion shows you respect the other person's perspective and expertise. That simple act can go a long way toward strengthening relationships and mutual respect.

Plus, it keeps us in a learning mindset. By staying open to feedback, we're signaling to others—and reminding ourselves—that there's always room to grow. And that inspires everyone involved to keep improving.

Last, treating suggestions as gifts and genuinely engaging with those around you shows that you're eager to learn and grow. It sends a clear message that you're open to feedback and committed to improving yourself. The key to real change, though, is consistency—people need to see it over time to truly believe it.

By seeking input from others, you're not just saying you value their opinions—you're also creating chances to demonstrate new behaviors that can shift their perception of you. And it's not just about listening; it's about taking action. When you actually apply the feedback you receive, people start to notice. Change isn't about one big moment—it's about the small, repeated actions that shape how others see you.

Following up is just as important. Checking in with people and asking if they've noticed a difference helps reinforce that you're serious about growth. Over time, this consistent effort reshapes how others perceive you, proving that you're truly committed to becoming your best self.

So the next time someone offers you a suggestion—whether it's part of the Feedforward process or not—try to see it for what it really is: a gift. Even if what they suggest isn't the right fit, just saying, "Thank you," can transform the whole dynamic. It's a small thing that makes a big difference.

Regular Use of Feedforward

The regular use of Feedforward is nothing short of transformative.

At work, during one-on-one meetings with team members, we use it to focus on what's ahead instead of dwelling on what's already happened. We'll ask things like, "What can we do better moving forward?" or "How can we support you in reaching your goals?" It's a great way to keep the conversation constructive and future-focused.

In team meetings, we take the same approach. We encourage everyone to share suggestions for the next steps on projects or strategies. This helps create a collaborative environment where the energy is focused on finding solutions and making progress.

Now, in your personal life, Feedforward is just as powerful. With family and friends, we'll ask for their thoughts on how we can be a better listener, a more supportive partner, or a more present parent. It shows them we value their perspectives, and it keeps us growing in ways that matter most to the people we care about.

And when someone we know wants to make a change, we try to offer Feedforward to them too—just a couple of positive, actionable suggestions they can use to move toward their goals. It's always about helping them look ahead, not back.

What's special about Feedforward is how it creates positive energy in any setting. It's a way to build trust, foster open communication, and keep everyone—including ourselves—focused on growth and improvement. Over time, it becomes second nature, and the results speak for themselves.

To us, Feedforward is so much more than just a tool. It's a way of thinking and interacting that can transform the way we grow, learn, and succeed. In our coaching, it's a key ingredient because it fosters a positive atmosphere for change, encourages continuous learning, and resonates deeply with those who are committed to improving their performance and achieving their goals.

And Feedforward works perfectly with Daily Questions. They're two sides of the same coin—both about moving forward, not dwelling on the past.

With Daily Questions, you hold yourself accountable by measuring your effort against your own standards every single day. With Feedforward, you get specific, future-focused advice on how to get better. You can even turn the suggestions you get from Feedforward into new Daily Questions!

This is all about shifting the focus from what went wrong to what you can do next—helping you develop and stick to the behaviors you want to keep to become the person you want to be.

So our challenge to you is this: Try this today.

- **Step 1:** Grab a friend, colleague, or family member.
- **Step 2:** Tell them briefly, in two to three minutes, about a goal you have.
- **Step 3:** Ask for their suggestions to help you improve or achieve your goal.
- **Step 4:** Say, "Thank you."

That's it! Now that you understand how Feedforward helps leaders focus on future possibilities and how to do it for yourself, the Wheel of Change is the next step. Feedforward gets you thinking about what you can do differently to grow and improve, and the Wheel of Change takes it further by giving you a clear framework to act on those insights. It'll help you see what you need to create in your life, recognize what's worth preserving, let go of what's holding you back, and make peace with the things you can't change. These tools work seamlessly together: Feedforward gets your momentum going, and the Wheel of Change helps make sure that momentum is balanced and purposeful. It's about making meaningful progress toward becoming the best version of yourself.

The Wheel of Change Model: Becoming the Best Version of the Future You

The Wheel of Change, from Marshall's book *Triggers*, is the model we use when helping someone figure out how to become the person they want to be. It's simple, and it's incredibly effective. It has two dimensions: Positive or Negative and Change or Keep. These dimensions go around in a circle in four quadrants: Creating, Preserving, Eliminating, and Accepting.

THE WHEEL OF CHANGE

Becoming the Person We Want to Become

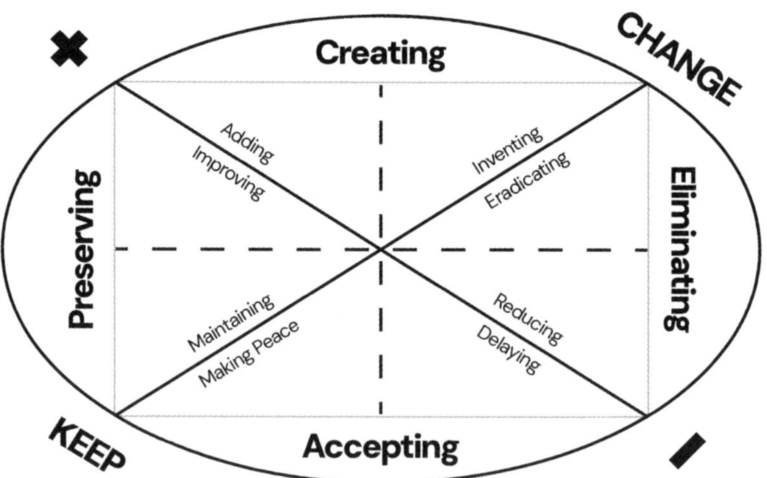

Creating

The first piece of this model is what we call Creating. Creating focuses on the positive elements you want to add to your life—new skills, habits, or relationships aligned with your future goals. It's about asking, *Who do I want to be? How is that version of me different from who I am today?* Then, you take actionable steps to make it permanent. It could mean developing new skills, forming healthier habits, or building new relationships that align with the life you want to create.

This part of the Wheel of Change is great because it's where self-invention happens. It's where you get to dream about what's possible and take conscious steps toward making that vision a reality. Whether it's in your career, your relationships, or your personal growth, this is where the change begins—the quadrant where you focus on creating a future that reflects your best self.

Two Key Dimensions

After the Creating stage, the Wheel of Change introduces two key dimensions: Positive or Negative and Change or Keep. These dimensions help us think through the areas of our lives that we need to address as we work toward becoming our future selves.

- **Positive or Negative**: This dimension is all about taking stock of what's working and what's not. The positive represents the things that help us move forward—the strengths, habits, and relationships that add value to our lives. The negative includes the things that hold us back—those behaviors, patterns, or even relationships that get in the way of our growth.

- **Change or Keep**: This dimension is about making choices. What are the things we want to change in our lives? And just as importantly, what do we want to keep exactly as they are? It's about being deliberate in deciding what to let go of and what to preserve.

Now, when you combine these dimensions, you get the four quadrants of the Wheel of Change:

1. **Creating (Positive Change)**: Introducing habits, behaviors, or relationships that help you grow.
2. **Preserving (Positive Keep)**: Recognizing and maintaining strengths and values that serve you well.
3. **Eliminating (Negative Change)**: Letting go of behaviors or relationships that hinder progress.
4. **Accepting (Negative Keep)**: Making peace with aspects you can't or won't change.

By working through each quadrant, you get a personalized, balanced plan for growth. The Wheel helps you focus on what you can create and preserve while eliminating what holds you back and accepting what you cannot—or choose not—to change. This process helps you take control of your journey to becoming the best version of yourself.

Identity and Creating

Then, inside the circle are what we call "elements." The first element is about making conscious choices for who we want to become in the future. We can be anyone we choose to be. The problem for most people is that we may not have *consciously* chosen how we see ourselves. Instead, how we see ourselves may have been shaped by messages we picked up along the way about who *others* believed we should be. If you came from a family where you had siblings, you may have gotten messages from them. Maybe you got the message at some point that you were "the smart one" or "the responsible one." These roles shape how we all see ourselves—no matter how successful we eventually become. Like Dr. Jim Kim—he's got a Harvard MD and PhD, he was the president of Dartmouth, and he is a cofounder of Partners In Health. Jim is an incredibly accomplished guy—he's the "smart one" in his sibling group—and even *he* carries identities he wrestles with. One time, Jim asked Marshall a question that really showed his brilliance: "How can I be better?" For someone as accomplished as Jim to be that curious, that humble, and that committed to improvement—that was impressive.

In getting to know Jim, Marshall realized this: Even for such a brilliant guy, it's hard not to go through life without struggling with identities we've taken on as a result of other people. The smart one, the responsible one, the funny one. The clever one, the pretty one. The athletic one, the nonathletic one. Whatever it is. In Jim's case, he didn't let that identity consume him. He also saw the value in seeking outside input so he could continually improve himself.

Just like Jim, you can be conscious of how you want to see yourself and present yourself. Think about the you that *you want to be* in the future. What is one little change you could make to how you identify yourself that would be helpful for you in the future? Maybe you're naturally responsible, but you don't *always* have to be responsible; you can loosen up, delegate, let some of that identity go. Maybe you're smart, but you don't always have to prove to everyone how smart you are. Or maybe you don't have to be the funny one all the time; you can let your serious side show when it feels appropriate. Whatever it is for you. You can ask yourself: Who do I see myself as, and how did I get this way? Your answers may surprise you.

Preserving the Positive

The second element of the Wheel of Change model is called Preserving. Preserving ensures we don't lose what's already working for us. We've told you about Frances Hesselbein and her leadership at the Girl Scouts. When Frances took over, the organization was in rough shape—membership was down, finances were tight, and membership didn't reflect the diversity of America's girls. Yet Frances knew she couldn't just scrap everything and start over. Instead, she embraced a simple, powerful philosophy: "Tradition with a future." She worked to modernize the organization—like having designer Bill Blass create new uniforms—while also honoring the past, letting scouts proudly keep wearing their old uniforms if they wanted to. That balance showed respect for the people who built the organization while creating space for what was next. We encourage other leaders to learn from her. CEOs especially, in their drive to transform their organizations, can risk showing disrespect for what came before.

The same applies to personal growth. As you think about who you want to become, don't forget to honor the parts of yourself that have served you well. The practice of Preserving invites you to ask yourself: What's worth keeping? Because sometimes, the key to moving forward is knowing what's worth bringing along.

Eliminating the Negative

The third element of the model is Eliminating. This one's all about identifying and letting go of the negative elements in your life—the behaviors, thoughts, habits, or relationships that are no longer serving you. This part of the Wheel asks you to make the conscious decision to say, "This isn't helping me anymore, and it's time to let it go." Eliminating can be incredibly liberating. There's something powerful about creating space for the new, positive changes you want to make by removing what isn't working. But let's be honest—it can also be tough. Sometimes what we need to eliminate is comfortable or familiar. Maybe it's a habit we've leaned on for years, a routine we've outgrown, or even a person whose presence is doing more harm than good. Letting go of these can feel hard, but it's essential for growth. So, Eliminating invites you to ask yourself: "What's weighing me down?"

Accepting Reality

And then finally, we want to spend some time on this very important part of the Wheel: Accepting. This aspect of personal growth is so important and often turns out to be the most challenging. It can also be the most liberating.

Acceptance involves recognizing and making peace with aspects of our lives that we cannot change. It's about asking ourselves: "What is it I need to make peace with?" This will be something you don't like that you also cannot change. What do you need to make peace with? Who do you need to forgive?

In Marshall's article "Lessons I Learned from Peter Drucker," he remembers Drucker telling him, "Our mission in life is to make a positive difference. Not to prove how smart we are, not to prove how right we are."* We so seldom in life remember this lesson. Think about it: How often do we find ourselves caught up in arguments just to prove how smart or right we are? It's a waste of time.

So here's what you can do instead. Ask yourself, "Am I willing to invest in making a positive difference?" Before engaging with any topic or situation, pause and ask yourself this question. If the answer is no, let it go. You'll be amazed at how this simple practice can transform your life and interactions. We waste so much of our lives dealing with topics where we are not going to make a difference. This drains our energy and distracts us from places where we could have a meaningful impact. By learning to accept what we cannot change and focusing our efforts on what we can, we can make a difference. This simple shift can lead to greater fulfillment, improved relationships, and more effective leadership.

Remember, acceptance doesn't mean giving up. It's about choosing our battles and focusing our energy on constructive change. As the last quadrant on the Wheel of Change, Acceptance is a reminder of the power we have to shape our lives by choosing what to embrace and what to let go.

The Wheel of Change gives you a road map for personal growth, but how do you decide who you want to become? That's where the Hero's Exercise comes in. It helps you identify the values and qualities you admire most—then challenges you to step into them yourself. By bridging the gap between admiration and action, this exercise turns inspiration into transformation, showing you how to embody the traits of the people you respect most.

---

* Marshall Goldsmith, "Lessons I Learned from Peter Drucker," Global Peter Drucker Forum, September 25, 2018, https://www.druckerforum.org/blog/lessons-i-learned-from-peter-drucker-by-marshall-goldsmith/.

The Hero's Exercise: Becoming the Person You Admire Most

Here's a simple but powerful idea: The people you look up to—their values, their strengths, the way they show up in the world—aren't just admirable. They're a mirror. They reflect the kind of person you *can* become. That's the whole point of the Hero's Exercise, a tool Marshall learned from his friend, designer Ayse Birsel.* It's a simple way to get clear on your values and aspirations while giving yourself permission to step into those qualities today.

Here's how it works:

1. **Write down the names of your heroes.** These can be real or fictional—historical figures, mentors, teachers, leaders, even characters from books or movies. Anyone who inspires you.
2. **Next to each name, list what you admire about them.** What makes them stand out? Is it their courage, integrity, kindness, resilience, creativity? Be specific.
3. **Now, cross out their names and replace them with your own.** Yes, really. This part can feel a little uncomfortable at first, but stay with it.
4. **Reflect on how you can bring these qualities into your own life.** What's one thing you can do today to live more like the people you admire?

That's it. Simple, right? But don't let the simplicity fool you—this is a mindset shift that can change everything.

---

* Ayse Birsel, *How to Design the Life You Love*, The Conversation Factory, March 27, 2020, https://theconversationfactory.com/podcast/how-to-design-the-life-you-love-ayse-birsel.

Most of us think of our heroes as somehow separate from us, as if they have something we don't. But the truth is, the reason you admire these qualities in others is because they *matter* to you. And if they matter to you, they're already inside you in some way. The Hero's Exercise helps bridge the gap between admiration and action.

Marshall used this process when he started the 100 Coaches project, where he decided to share everything he knew for free with other coaches, knowing they'd pay it forward. He saw generosity and mentorship in his own heroes, and instead of just admiring it, he *became* it.

So, who are your heroes? And more importantly—when do you start living like them?

We're nearing end of this book, and this is where the real work begins. Sustainable success isn't about big breakthroughs or dramatic changes—it's about the small, steady actions that keep you moving in the right direction. Daily Questions and self-reflection aren't just concepts; they're the habits that build a life of purpose, growth, and accountability. Whether you're leading a team, moving up in your career, or simply trying to be a better version of yourself, the key isn't just reaching your goals—it's keeping the momentum going. Keep measuring what matters, stay open to feedback, and surround yourself with the right people. That's permanence.

KEY PRINCIPLES OF

Feedforward

1. Focus on the Future

Avoid discussing past mistakes to reduce defensiveness and negativity.

Accept suggestions positively with a simple "Thank you" to foster openness.

2. Treat Suggestions as Gifts

View feedback as thoughtful contributions that build trust and collaboration.

Emphasize possibilities over criticism to encourage creativity and learning.

3. Use Feedforward Regularly

- Apply it in work meetings to focus on future improvements.
- Use it in personal relationships to enhance support and presence.
- Encourage actionable suggestions to maintain growth-focused interactions.

4. Positive Impact

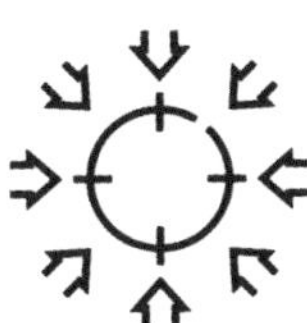

Builds trust, energy, and momentum by focusing on goals and next steps.

Avoids dwelling on mistakes and fosters constructive progress.

5. The Hero's Exercise

- List the names of your heroes.
- Next to each, list what you admire about them.
- Cross out the names and replace with your own.
- Reflect on how you would bring what you admire about them into your own life.

6. Encourage Growth

Feedforward creates a positive, growth-oriented atmosphere.

Focus on future actions to unlock progress and long-term success.

THE WHEEL OF

Change

1. Creating Positive Change

Add new skills, habits, or relationships aligned with your goals.

Ask: Who do I want to be? What steps can I take to start creating that version?

2. Preserving Positives

Identify and maintain strengths, values, or traditions that serve you.

Ask: What's worth keeping in my current self or life?

3. Eliminating Negatives

Let go of habits, behaviors, or relationships that hinder growth.

Ask: What's holding me back, and what can I release?

 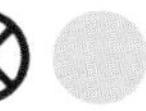    

4. Accepting the Unchangeable

Make peace with what cannot change.

Ask: What can I accept or forgive to move forward peacefully?

5. Two Dimensions of Change and Keep

Balance that which you should keep versus what you should let go of in your life.

6. Balanced Growth Road Map

Use the Wheel of Change to plan thoughtfully, blending new possibilities with reality.

Ask: Am I ready to invest in positive change? If not, let it go.

Epilogue

So here's some advice. Imagine you're ninety-five. You're on your deathbed, and here comes your last breath. Right before you take your last breath, you're given a beautiful gift—the ability to go back in time and talk to the people you love. The ability to help someone have a better life. What advice would the wise ninety-five-year-old you have for the you who is reading these words right now? You don't have to say anything or do anything. Just answer that question in your mind. Whatever you're thinking right now, do that. Some friends interviewed older folks and asked them this question: "What advice would you have?"

The first bit of advice? "Be happy now." Not next week, not next year, not next month. Be happy now. Get over the Great Western Disease of "I'll be happy when . . ." When I get the money, the status, the BMW. Get over it. Happiness is a choice, not a consequence of circumstances.

The second bit of advice—and this is a point President Bill Clinton once made—when you're ninety-five years old and you look around at the people gathered around that deathbed, none of your coworkers are waving goodbye. Your friends and family are there. They are the people are in your life who are most important.

The third bit of advice: If you have a personal dream, go for it. Because if you don't go for it when you're thirty-five, you may not when you're forty-five, and you probably won't when you're eighty-five. It doesn't have to be a big one. Maybe a little one. Go to New Zealand, speak Spanish, play the guitar. Other people may think your dream is goofy. Who cares? It's not their dream. It's yours. It's not their life; it's your life. On the business side, the advice is the same: Go for it. Your world's changing. Do what you think is right. You might not win, but you can look the mirror and say, "At least I tried."

The fourth bit of advice—and this is a blessing we all have—is to do whatever you can to help people. The main reason to help people has nothing to do with money or status or getting ahead. The main reason to help people is much deeper. The ninety-five-year-old you will be proud of you because you did, and they'll be disappointed if you don't. Take a cue from the Buddhists: One day we're all going to be equally dead, so we might as well do a little good while we're here.

A final thing we would like to say is it's our honor that you would spend your time here in these pages. We hope in our time together we've taught you something that's positive, practical, and useful. And hopefully it's helped you have a life that's just a little bit better.

Thank you very much.

Appendix: Supporting Studies and Research

1. Goldsmith, Marshall. "Which Workplace Habits Do You Need to Break to Become More Successful." *Journal for Quality and Participation* 30, no. 2 (2007): 4–8. https://www.proquest.com/docview/219108488?pq-origsite=gscholar&fromopenview=true&sourcetype=Scholarly%20Journals.
2. Goldsmith, Marshall. "Leadership Development: Try Feedforward instead of Feedback." *Journal of Excellence,* no. 8 (2003): 15–19. http://www.zoneofexcellence.ca/Journal/Issue08/Leadership.pdf.
3. Goldsmith, Marshall. "Questions That Make a Difference: The Daily Question Process." Marshall Goldsmith.com. https://marshallgoldsmith.com/articles/questions-that-make-a-difference-the-daily-question-process/.
4. Goldsmith, Marshall. "Helping People Achieve Their Goals." Marshall Goldsmith.com. March 31, 2014. https://marshallgoldsmith.com/articles/helping-people-achieve-their-goals/.
5. Goldsmith, Marshall and Howard Morgan. "Leadership Is a Contact Sport: The 'Follow-up Factor' in Management Development." *Strategy+Business*. August 25, 2004. https://www.strategy-business.com/article/04307.

Daily Questions Journal

"Answer six questions for two minutes a day and you can change almost anything."

*"Anybody can change,
but they have to want to change."*

—MARSHALL GOLDSMITH

Day 1		1=No	2
1.	Did I do my best to set clear goals?		
2.	Did I do my best to make progress toward achieving my own goals?		
3.	Did I do my best to find meaning?		
4.	Did I do my best to be happy?		
5.	Did I do my best to build positive relationships?		
6.	Did I do my best to make progress toward goal achievement?		
7.			
8.			
9.			
10.			
11.			
12.			
13.			
14.			
15.			

Notes:

"The simplest tool I know to finding fulfillment is being open to fulfillment."

—MARSHALL GOLDSMITH

3	4	5	6	7	8	9	10=Yes

"Change is not a one-way street—it involves two parties: the person who is changing and the people who notice it."

—MARSHALL GOLDSMITH

Day 2		1=No	2
1.	Did I do my best to set clear goals?		
2.	Did I do my best to make progress toward achieving my own goals?		
3.	Did I do my best to find meaning?		
4.	Did I do my best to be happy?		
5.	Did I do my best to build positive relationships?		
6.	Did I do my best to make progress toward goal achievement?		
7.			
8.			
9.			
10.			
11.			
12.			
13.			
14.			
15.			

Notes:

"A wise person learns from their mistakes—a much wiser person learns from someone else's mistakes."

—MARSHALL GOLDSMITH

3	4	5	6	7	8	9	10=Yes

"Great leaders encourage leadership development by openly developing themselves."

—MARSHALL GOLDSMITH

Day 3		1=No	2
1.	Did I do my best to set clear goals?		
2.	Did I do my best to make progress toward achieving my own goals?		
3.	Did I do my best to find meaning?		
4.	Did I do my best to be happy?		
5.	Did I do my best to build positive relationships?		
6.	Did I do my best to make progress toward goal achievement?		
7.			
8.			
9.			
10.			
11.			
12.			
13.			
14.			
15.			

Notes:

*"Fate is the hand of cards we've been dealt.
Choice is how we play the hand."*

—MARSHALL GOLDSMITH

3	4	5	6	7	8	9	10=Yes

"If we do not create and control our environment, our environment creates and controls us."

—MARSHALL GOLDSMITH

Day 4		1=No	2
1.	Did I do my best to set clear goals?		
2.	Did I do my best to make progress toward achieving my own goals?		
3.	Did I do my best to find meaning?		
4.	Did I do my best to be happy?		
5.	Did I do my best to build positive relationships?		
6.	Did I do my best to make progress toward goal achievement?		
7.			
8.			
9.			
10.			
11.			
12.			
13.			
14.			
15.			

Notes:

"Successful people become great leaders when they learn to shift the focus from themselves to others."

—MARSHALL GOLDSMITH

3	4	5	6	7	8	9	10=Yes

"Improvement is hard. If it were easy, we'd already be better."

—MARSHALL GOLDSMITH

Day 5		1=No	2
1.	Did I do my best to set clear goals?		
2.	Did I do my best to make progress toward achieving my own goals?		
3.	Did I do my best to find meaning?		
4.	Did I do my best to be happy?		
5.	Did I do my best to build positive relationships?		
6.	Did I do my best to make progress toward goal achievement?		
7.			
8.			
9.			
10.			
11.			
12.			
13.			
14.			
15.			

Notes:

"The greatest challenge in behavioral change is not knowing what to do—the greatest challenge is doing it!"

—MARSHALL GOLDSMITH

3	4	5	6	7	8	9	10=Yes

"It is a whole lot easier to see our problems in others than it is to see them in ourselves."

—MARSHALL GOLDSMITH

Day 6		1=No	2
1.	Did I do my best to set clear goals?		
2.	Did I do my best to make progress toward achieving my own goals?		
3.	Did I do my best to find meaning?		
4.	Did I do my best to be happy?		
5.	Did I do my best to build positive relationships?		
6.	Did I do my best to make progress toward goal achievement?		
7.			
8.			
9.			
10.			
11.			
12.			
13.			
14.			
15.			

Notes:

"The most reliable predictor of what you will be doing five minutes from now is what you are doing now."

—MARSHALL GOLDSMITH

3	4	5	6	7	8	9	10=Yes

"Leadership is not about me. It is all about them."

—MARSHALL GOLDSMITH

Day 7		1=No	2
1.	Did I do my best to set clear goals?		
2.	Did I do my best to make progress toward achieving my own goals?		
3.	Did I do my best to find meaning?		
4.	Did I do my best to be happy?		
5.	Did I do my best to build positive relationships?		
6.	Did I do my best to make progress toward goal achievement?		
7.			
8.			
9.			
10.			
11.			
12.			
13.			
14.			
15.			

Notes:

"Gratitude is not a limited resource, nor is it costly. It is abundant as air. We breathe it in but forget to exhale."

—MARSHALL GOLDSMITH

3	4	5	6	7	8	9	10=Yes

"People who believe they can succeed see opportunities where others see threats."

—MARSHALL GOLDSMITH

Day 8		1=No	2
1.	Did I do my best to set clear goals?		
2.	Did I do my best to make progress toward achieving my own goals?		
3.	Did I do my best to find meaning?		
4.	Did I do my best to be happy?		
5.	Did I do my best to build positive relationships?		
6.	Did I do my best to make progress toward goal achievement?		
7.			
8.			
9.			
10.			
11.			
12.			
13.			
14.			
15.			

Notes:

"Whether you're leading other people or leading the follower in you, the obstacles to achieving your goals are the same."

—MARSHALL GOLDSMITH

3	4	5	6	7	8	9	10=Yes

"To help others develop, start with yourself."

—MARSHALL GOLDSMITH

Day 9		1=No	2
1.	Did I do my best to set clear goals?		
2.	Did I do my best to make progress toward achieving my own goals?		
3.	Did I do my best to find meaning?		
4.	Did I do my best to be happy?		
5.	Did I do my best to build positive relationships?		
6.	Did I do my best to make progress toward goal achievement?		
7.			
8.			
9.			
10.			
11.			
12.			
13.			
14.			
15.			

Notes:

"Five qualities that you need to bring to an activity in order to do it well are motivation, knowledge, ability, confidence, and authenticity."

—MARSHALL GOLDSMITH

3	4	5	6	7	8	9	10=Yes

"Treat every piece of advice as a gift or a compliment and simply say, 'Thank you.'"

—MARSHALL GOLDSMITH

Day 10		1=No	2
1.	Did I do my best to set clear goals?		
2.	Did I do my best to make progress toward achieving my own goals?		
3.	Did I do my best to find meaning?		
4.	Did I do my best to be happy?		
5.	Did I do my best to build positive relationships?		
6.	Did I do my best to make progress toward goal achievement?		
7.			
8.			
9.			
10.			
11.			
12.			
13.			
14.			
15.			

Notes:

"If we can stop, listen, and think about what others are seeing in us, we have a great opportunity."

—MARSHALL GOLDSMITH

3	4	5	6	7	8	9	10=Yes

"When we do what we have to do, we are compliant. When we do what we choose to do, we are committed."

—MARSHALL GOLDSMITH

Day 11		1=No	2
1.	Did I do my best to set clear goals?		
2.	Did I do my best to make progress toward achieving my own goals?		
3.	Did I do my best to find meaning?		
4.	Did I do my best to be happy?		
5.	Did I do my best to build positive relationships?		
6.	Did I do my best to make progress toward goal achievement?		
7.			
8.			
9.			
10.			
11.			
12.			
13.			
14.			
15.			

Notes:

"Leadership is providing inspiration and vision, then developing and empowering others to achieve this vision."

—MARSHALL GOLDSMITH

3	4	5	6	7	8	9	10=Yes

"Life is short. Do whatever you can to help people."

—MARSHALL GOLDSMITH

Day 12		1=No	2
1.	Did I do my best to set clear goals?		
2.	Did I do my best to make progress toward achieving my own goals?		
3.	Did I do my best to find meaning?		
4.	Did I do my best to be happy?		
5.	Did I do my best to build positive relationships?		
6.	Did I do my best to make progress toward goal achievement?		
7.			
8.			
9.			
10.			
11.			
12.			
13.			
14.			
15.			

Notes:

"The best way that we can begin to produce positive change is to make peace with what is in ourselves."

—MARSHALL GOLDSMITH

3	4	5	6	7	8	9	10=Yes

"If you know what matters to you, it's easier to commit to change."

—MARSHALL GOLDSMITH

Day 13		1=No	2
1.	Did I do my best to set clear goals?		
2.	Did I do my best to make progress toward achieving my own goals?		
3.	Did I do my best to find meaning?		
4.	Did I do my best to be happy?		
5.	Did I do my best to build positive relationships?		
6.	Did I do my best to make progress toward goal achievement?		
7.			
8.			
9.			
10.			
11.			
12.			
13.			
14.			
15.			

Notes:

"Those who lead by example and demonstrate passion for what they do make it much easier for their followers to do the same."

—MARSHALL GOLDSMITH

3	4	5	6	7	8	9	10=Yes

"Getting better is its own reward. If we do that, we can never feel cheated."

—MARSHALL GOLDSMITH

Day 14		1=No	2
1.	Did I do my best to set clear goals?		
2.	Did I do my best to make progress toward achieving my own goals?		
3.	Did I do my best to find meaning?		
4.	Did I do my best to be happy?		
5.	Did I do my best to build positive relationships?		
6.	Did I do my best to make progress toward goal achievement?		
7.			
8.			
9.			
10.			
11.			
12.			
13.			
14.			
15.			

Notes:

"Mojo is that positive spirit toward what we are doing now that starts from the inside and radiates to the outside."

—MARSHALL GOLDSMITH

3	4	5	6	7	8	9	10=Yes

About the Authors

Lisa Broderick is a seasoned C-suite executive, corporate board member, and nonprofit founder with three decades of leadership experience across diverse industries, blending science with personal transformation. Author of the international bestseller *All the Time in the World*, which was translated into dozens of languages, and a frequent contributor to *Psychology Today*, Lisa distills human behavior, science, and systems thinking into complex organizational and behavioral insights. Her books deliver practical, results-driven strategies that empower individuals and organizations to achieve lasting success.

Dr. Marshall Goldsmith is a world-renowned business educator and executive coach, a member of the Thinkers50 Hall of Fame, and the only two-time #1 leadership thinker in the world. He is a #1 *New York Times* bestselling author, having sold over four million copies and published in thirty-six languages. His *New York Times* bestsellers are: *What Got You Here Won't Get You There*, *Mojo*, *Triggers*, and *The Earned Life*. Marshall's clients have included over two hundred major CEOs and multiple leaders who have been recognized as CEO of the Year in the United States. His current mission is to share all that he knows with as many people as he can around the world.